LAYERING

AN ART OF TIME AND SPACE

*"...the relationships in art
are not necessarily ones of
outward form, but are founded
on inner sympathy of meaning."*

Wassily Kandinsky

**A SELECTION OF ART FROM MEMBERS
OF THE SOCIETY OF LAYERISTS IN MULTI MEDIA**

LAYERING

Layering is an art process that grows from a holistic worldview. Layerists concur that their layering process is a meditative route to another dimension, a time outside of time, a space beyond the three-dimensional, where they more readily perceive infinite, meaningful relationships. Through their artwork, layerists refer to those intersections that link apparently separate incidents and places, both in reality and in the mind. Independently, but mutually, these artists have developed a unified perspective of time and space. Layering is an expression of an apparent yearning in our American culture for reconnection with nature and a resacralization of our environment.

I coined the term Layering in the early 1970s. In the years since, layerists have enlarged their use of the word to refer not only to holism but also to healing through art. Reflecting the metaphysical adage, "As above, so be-low," layerists attempt to resolve the chaos of possibilities in their artwork, to make whole or heal the work of art. In doing so, they hope to heal themselves and, possibly, others. By presenting this collection of layered art in book form, we offer viewers an opportunity to perceive and benefit from its holistic intention.

Mary Carroll Nelson
Founder, SLMM, 1982

Layering is a term which has been appropriated by our society of artists because it best describes the process that all of us embrace in our search for dynamic form. This metaphor informs a particular working attitude. It recognizes the benefit of creating an expressive work which relies on layers of meaning that together reveal, as well as conceal, our perceptions and beliefs. These layers may be physical or conceptual but their aim is to bring density, resonance and "vital import" to the work that they animate.

Viewing artistic expression as a layering process allows us to find interconnectedness with all dimensions of life and our natural environment. We conceive art to be a rich healing force and process. The works we produce record our struggle to find a turning point of balance; one that keeps us constantly warmed by the sun's rays without separating us from the fertile depths of our mind's undergrowth. We realize that our artistic activity should be primarily directed toward self enrichment, spiritual awareness and social consciousness. If it honors these goals, it will also be dedicated to the care of the earth and act to heal those splits that threaten to obscure the oneness of being and the continuum of space/time.

Richard Newman
President, The Socety
of Layerists in Muti-Media

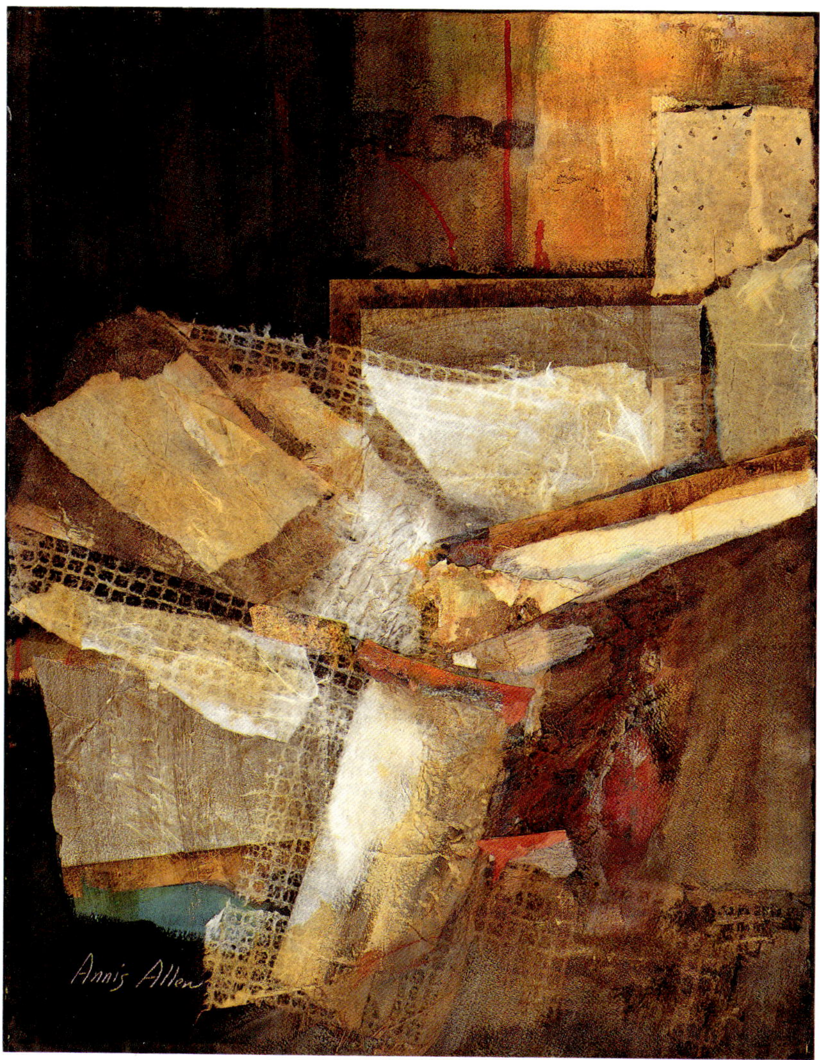

Photo: Jeff Rowe

ANNIS ALLEN

Metamorphosis
Mixed media collage
30 x 22 Inches

*Many of my paintings contain second hand objects.
It is my message that we must re-use and recycle,
in order to give our earth a chance to breathe.*

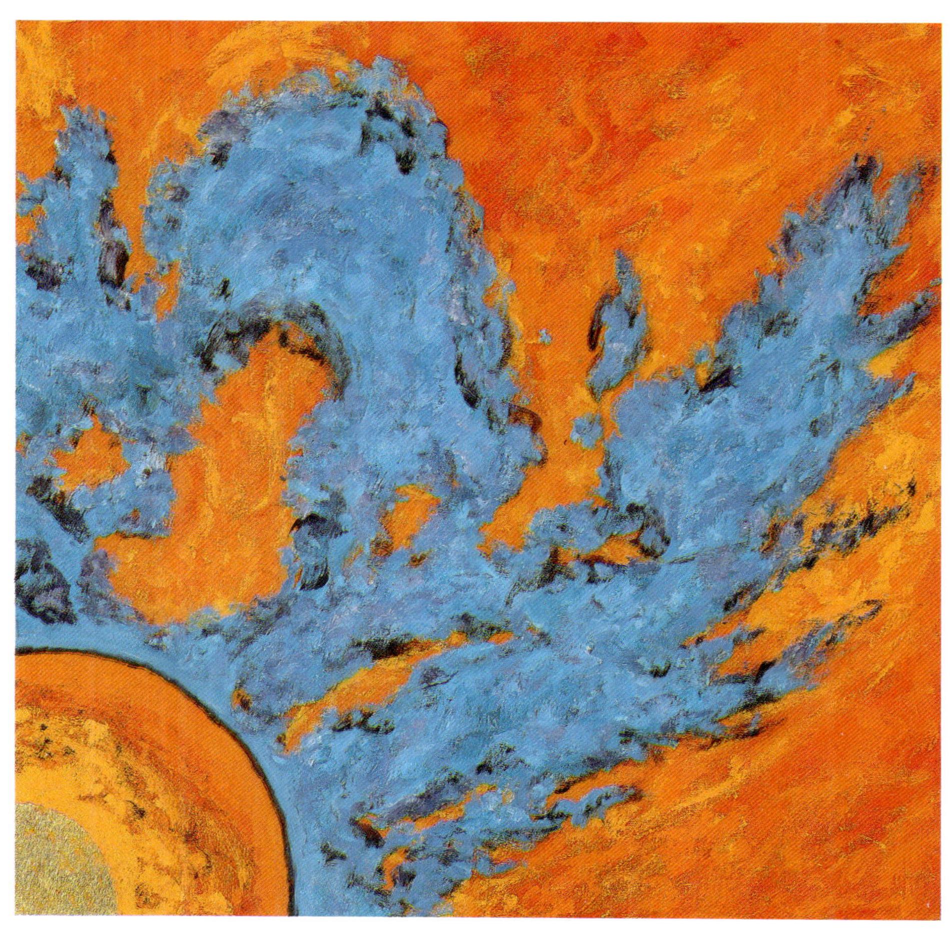

JUDY ASBURY

The Sun of Awareness
Oil and gold leaf on canvas
24x 24 Inches

My art expresses my feelings of being Gaia and part of the cosmos. This work has a spiritual motivation that originates from my concern, love and respect for Mother Earth.

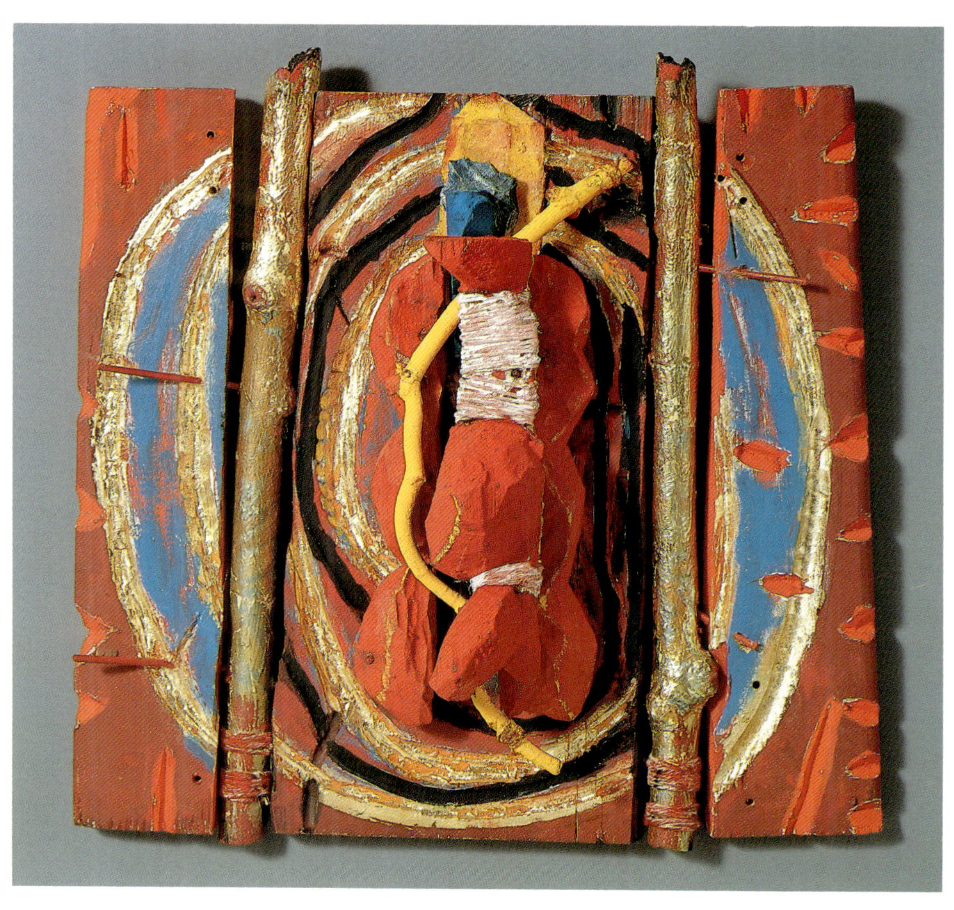

NANCY AZARA

Goddess Dream

Carved and painted wood with gold leaf
13 x 14 x 3 Inches

*I believe in the magical qualities and healing properties
inherent in art - making. My sculptures and artist books
are a visual description of the unseen and unknown,
a manifestation of our consciousness.*

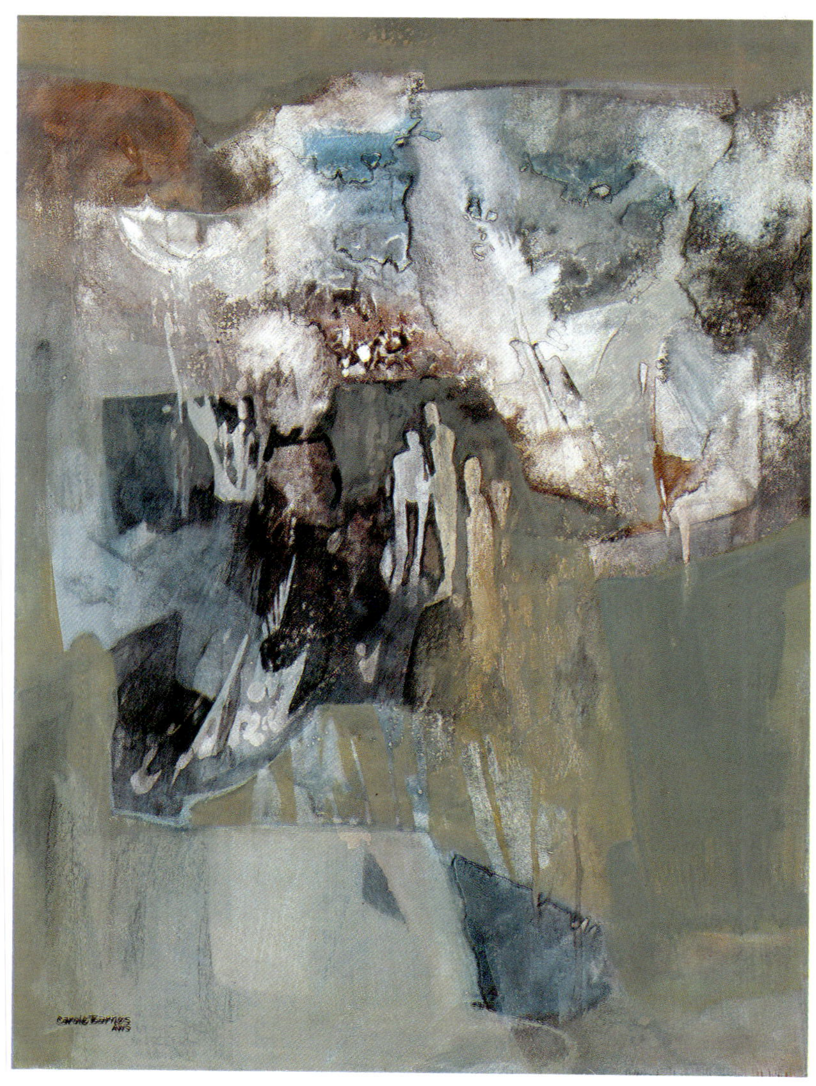

CAROLE D. BARNES

Ancestors of Antiquity

Acrylic
22 x 30 Inches

My work is involved with antiquity. I began with a personal digging. This soon evolved into a communication with a universal past, its people and its symbols both real and imagined.

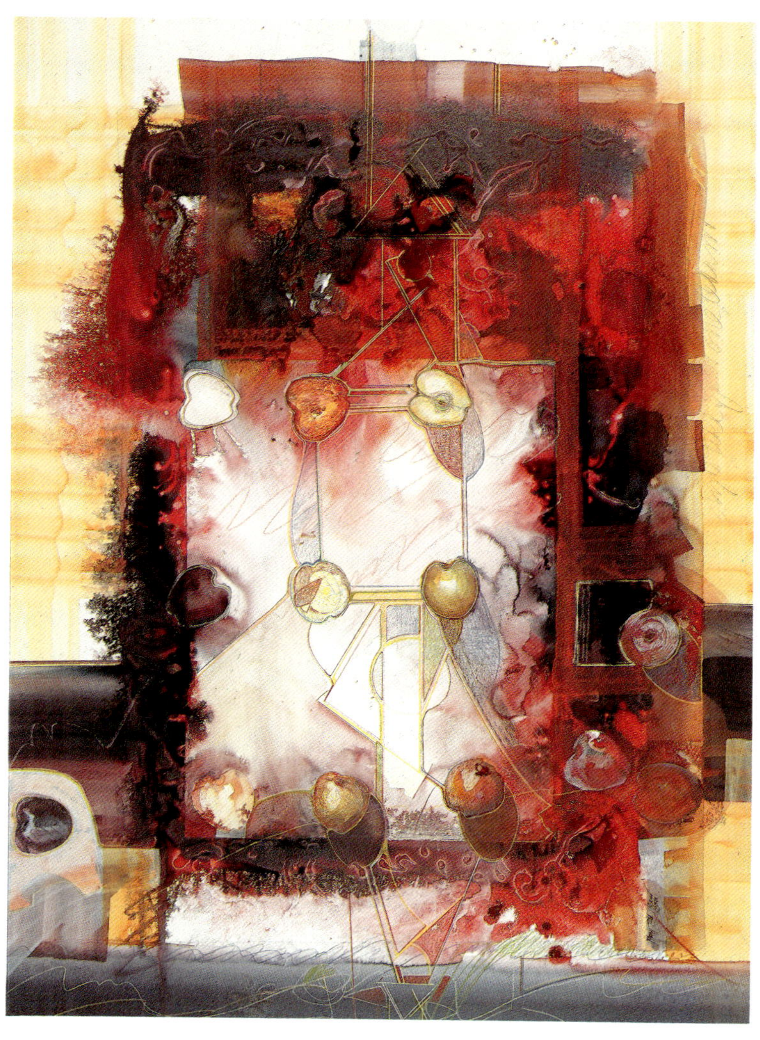

MARY TODD BEAM

Sacred Circuit
Mixed media
60 x 40 Inches

My work is an effort to affirm and celebrate the spiritual in art. From expressing and releasing pain, the soul is healed. In creativity, health and the spiritual are joined.

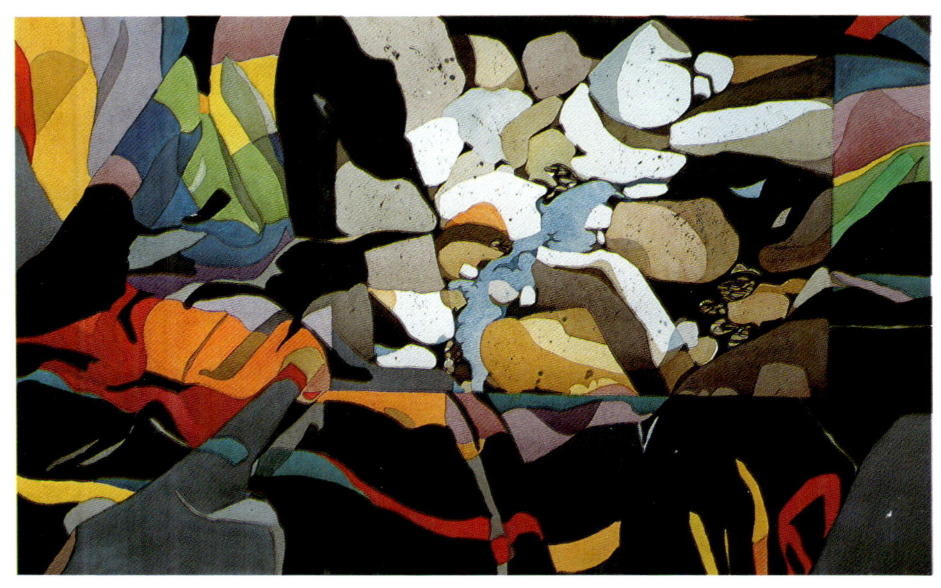

SANDRA E. BEEBE

Tidepools and Beachtowel
Transparent watercolor
22 x 30 Inches

I "gather", by hand and eye, arranging, controlling, designing litter, palettes, landscape elements using the beachtowel as basis for line to line, pulsating color, a perceptual layering, personal, dynamic, honest.

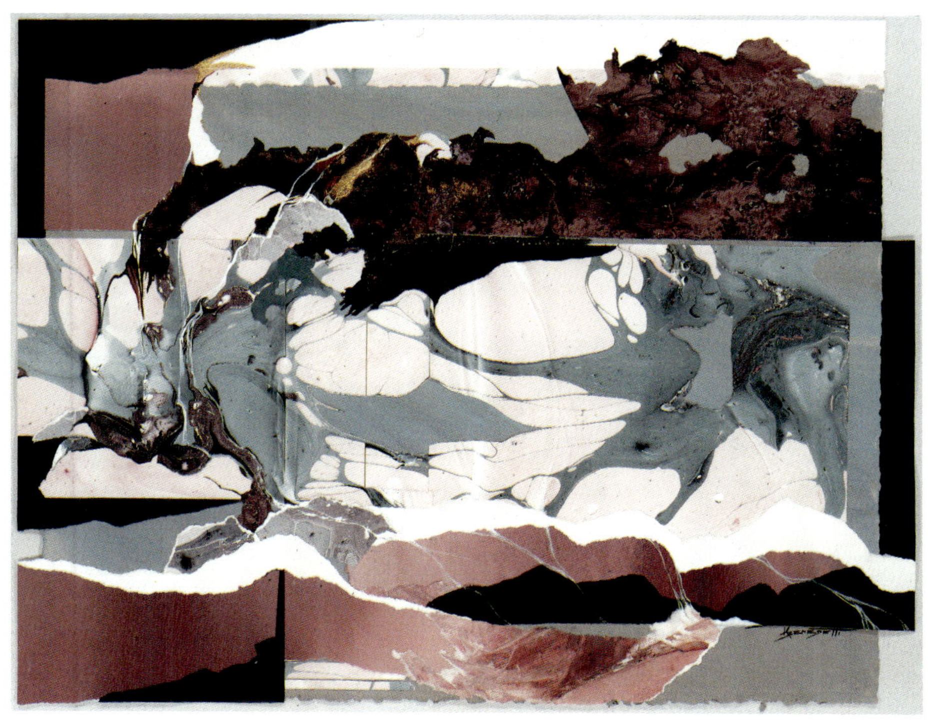

KAREN BECKER BENEDETTI

Earth's Fragmentation
Marbelized paper, acrylic, watercolor and
gold leaf
35 x 40 Inches

*Marbelized paper, poured acrylic and other
painted papers are combined to symbolize
earth's layered strata; as compared to the
evolutionary layering of civilizations, our own
being the most recent contribution.*

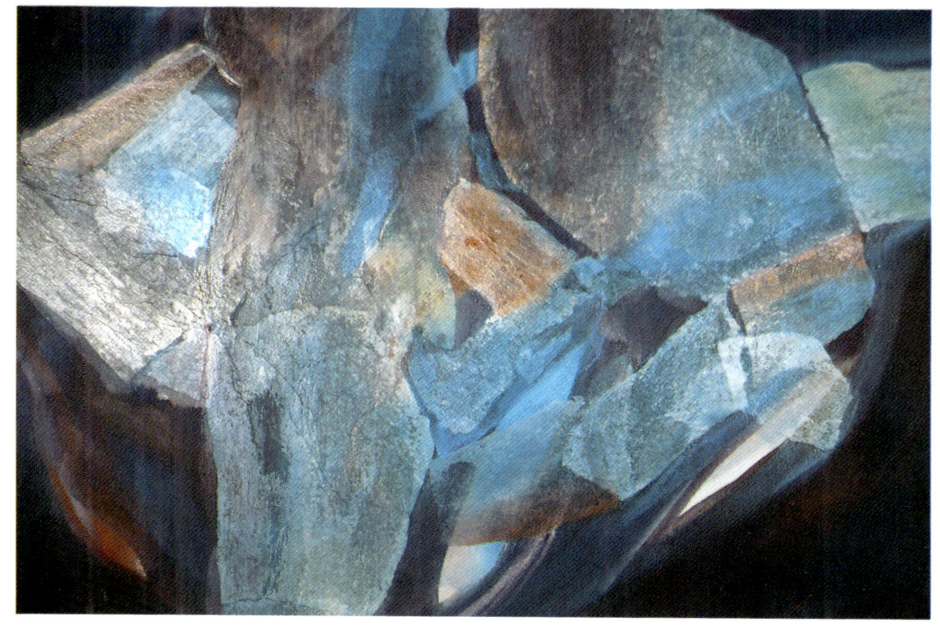

DOROTHEA M. BLUCK

Energy Source
Watercolor collage
22 x 30 Inches

*The layers of my work are to me symbols
of things that have gone before my time,
things of the present and the ongoing
future which will eventually lead to a higher
state of evolvement.*

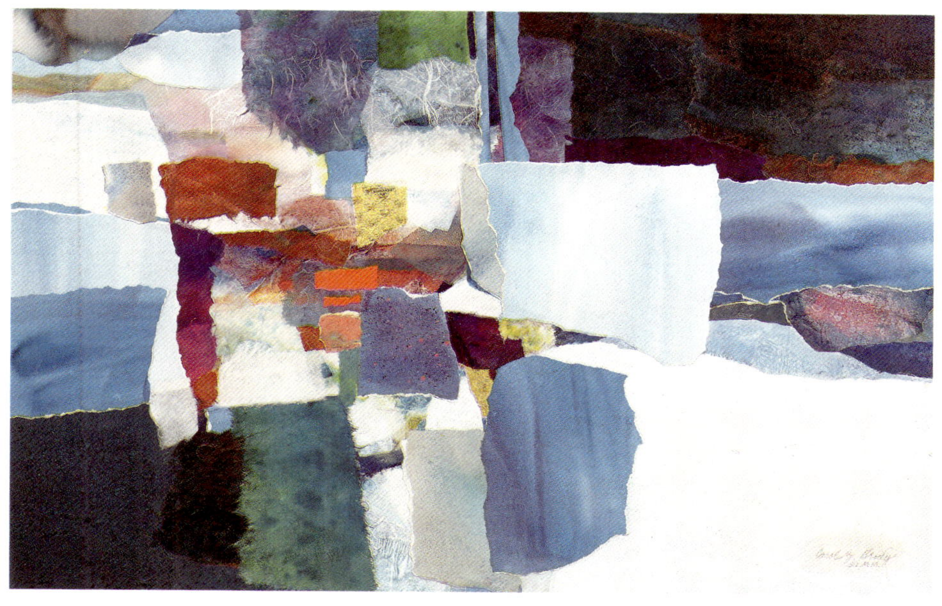

CAROL Z. BRODY

Candy Wrapper Series III
Watercolor, acrylic, various papers,
candy wrapper
20 x 30 Inches

*Layering imitates life. The mature work is
a synthesis of all the bits and pieces of
earlier stages. They enrich and embellish,
adding subtle colorations and deeper
meanings.*

PEGGY BROWN

Beneath the Waves
Watercolor and graphite pencil
29 x 39 Inches

*By expressing what is only in my mind, I hope
to connect my feelings with those of the
viewer in a more realistic way than I could
by painting realism.*

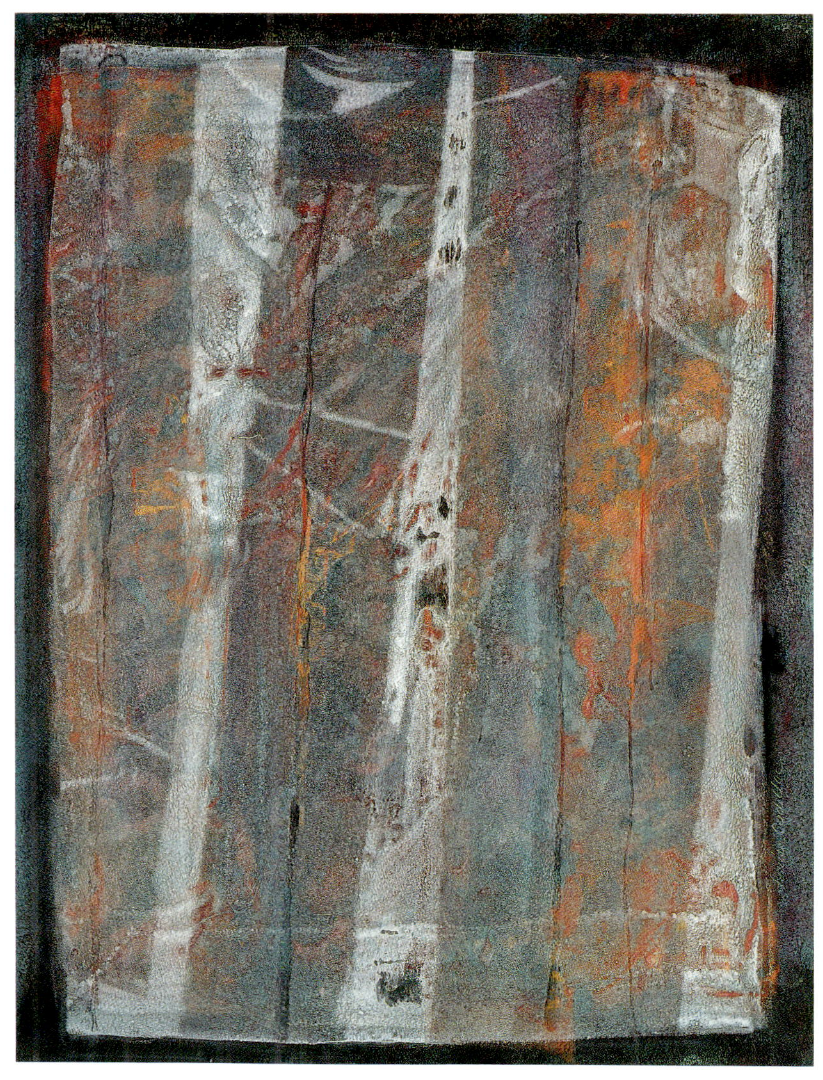

LOUISE CADILLAC

Ritual IX

Acrylic

30 x 22 Inches

The formal exploration of space and surface treatment as elements of emotional and intellectual power is constant in my work; a search for effective contemporary expression.

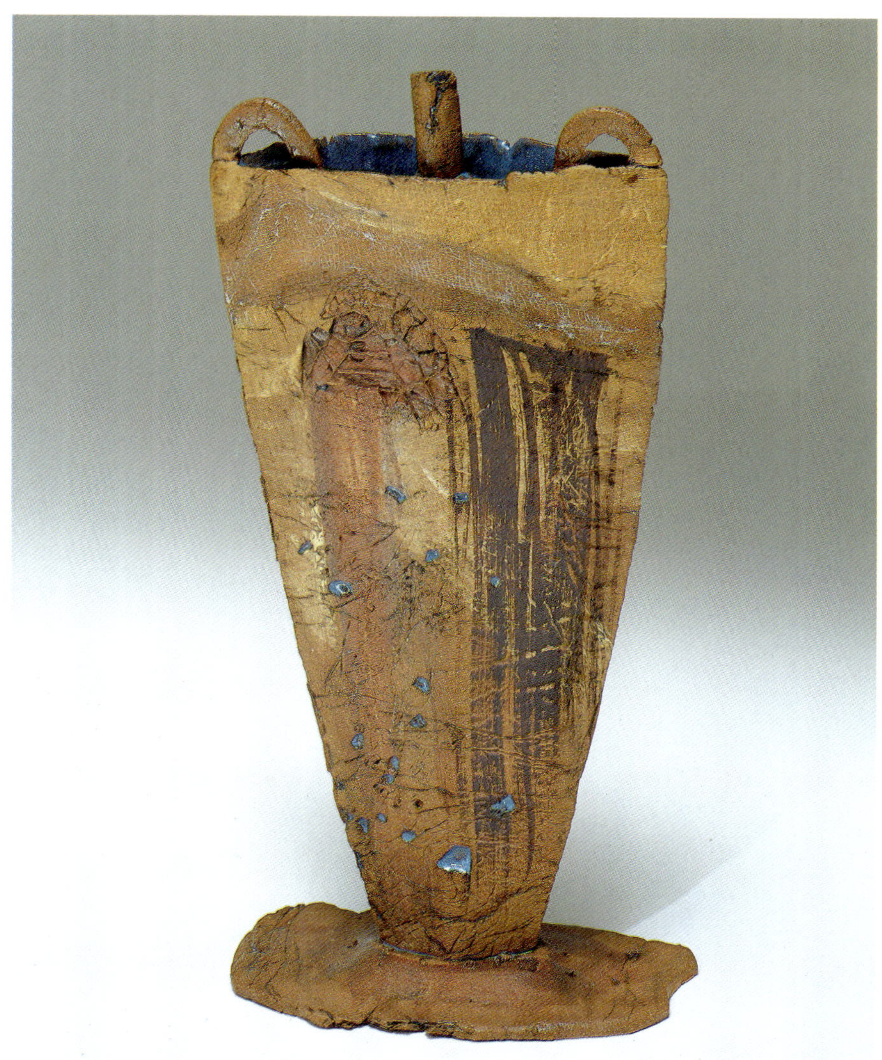

Photo: Damian Andrus

MARILYN CHRISTENSON

Rising Vessel
Stoneware
14 x 7 x 4 Inches

Classical vessel form, wood and volcanic ash, dry clay and oxides, combine to tell a story of geology, archaeology and spirit. Cool blue pools of glaze create tension and contrast.

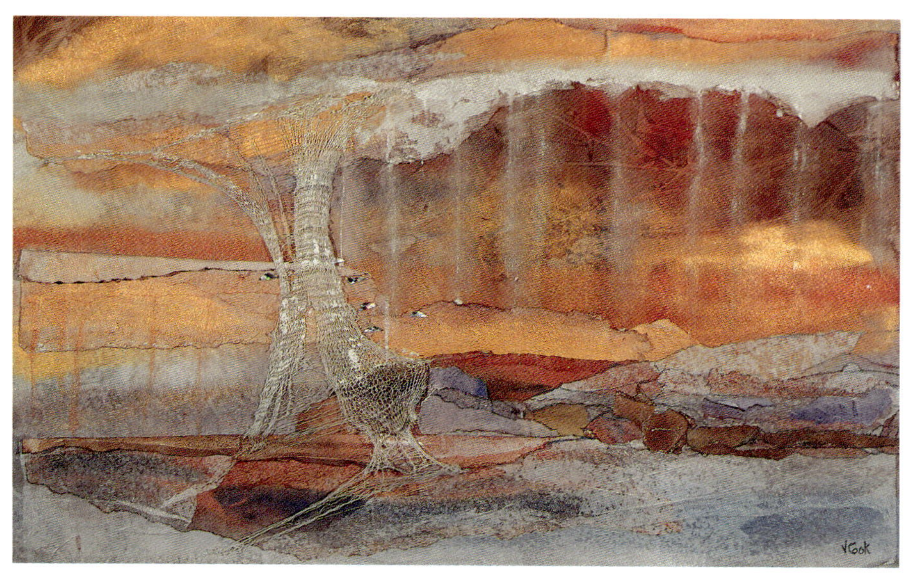

JANE COOK

Underwater Beauty
Watercolor collage
29 1/2 x 19 Inches

I paint from memory and from observing nature.
I also feel much of my inspiration comes from
unexplained motivations and I find this most
satisfying as an artist.

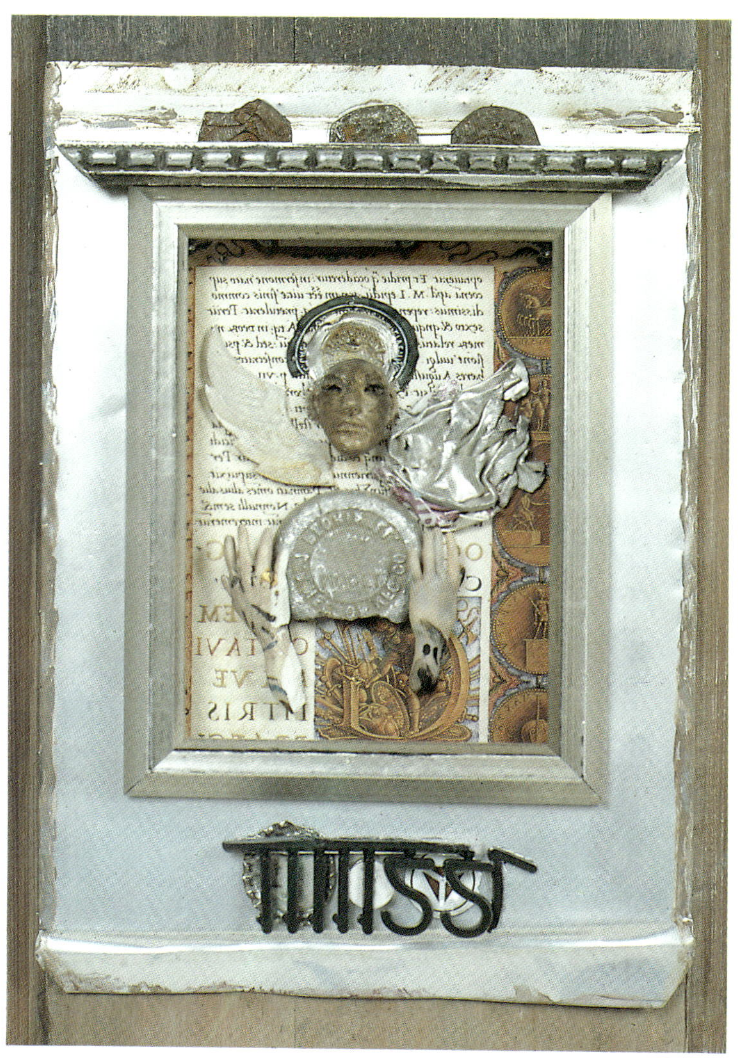

PAT COX

Shrine for an Unknown Object
Assemblage
19 1/2 x 14 x 2 Inches

My work explores the mystery and power of found objects through combination, alteration, juxtaposition and layering. The goal: transformation... the ordinary into the extraordinary, the frog into the prince.

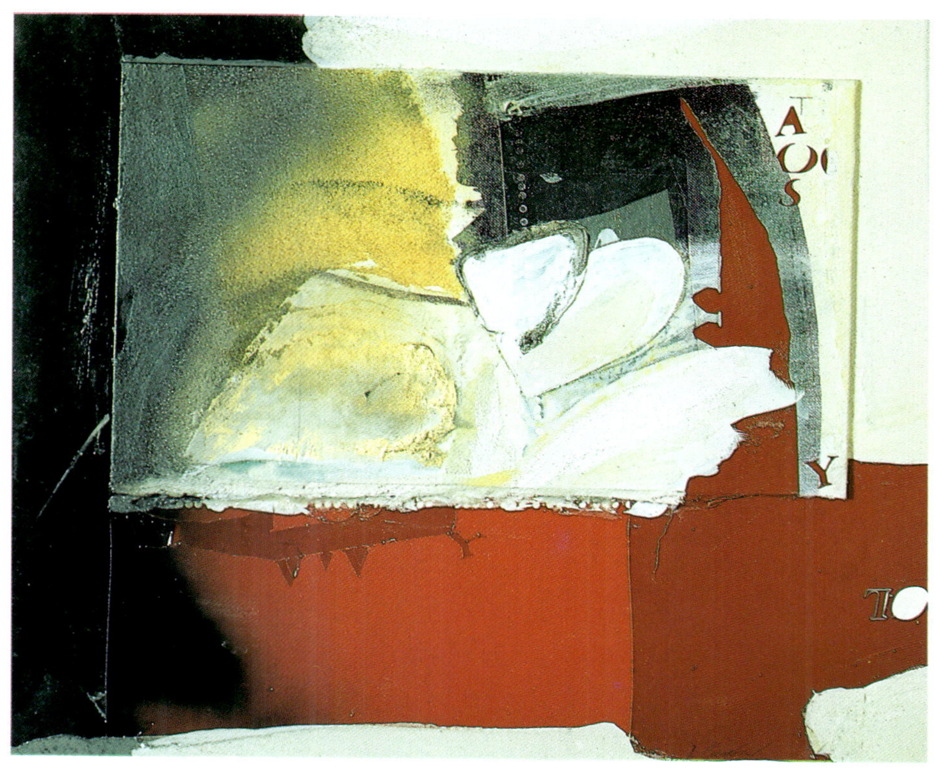

LESLIE CRESPIN

Thoughts of Taos
Mixed media
21 x 18 Inches

What I find appealing is combining objects of the past with the present to create possibilities for the future in my work. Hoping the observer can travel with me, through different experiences.

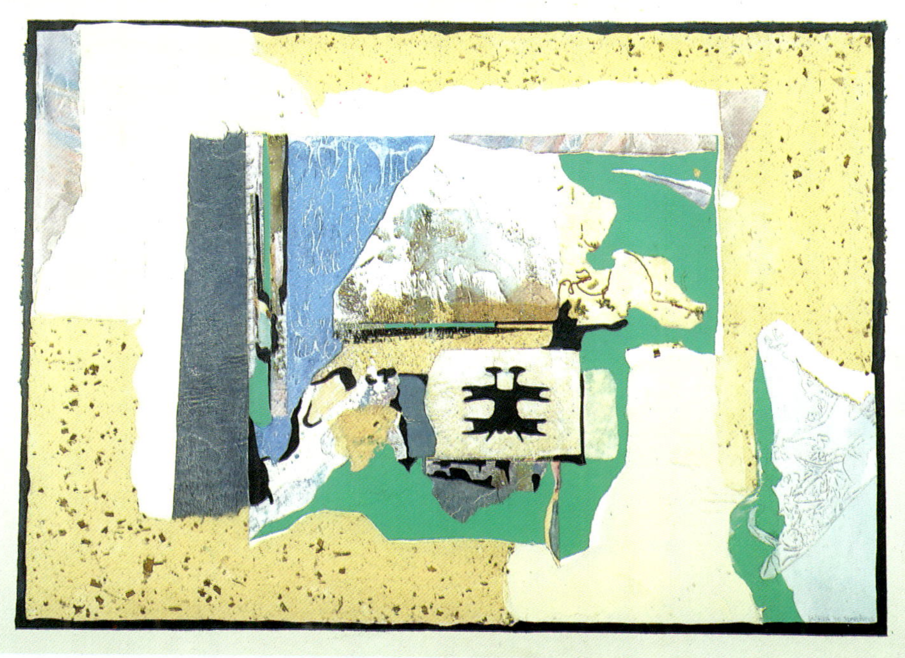

VALAIDA D'ALESSIO

Shaman Journey
Mixed media collage on canvas
48 x 36 Inches

*My paintings are intuitive, complex, a
release of emotions. They are personal,
my identity, an area of life controlled by
no one but myself. They are each a
personal journey within.*

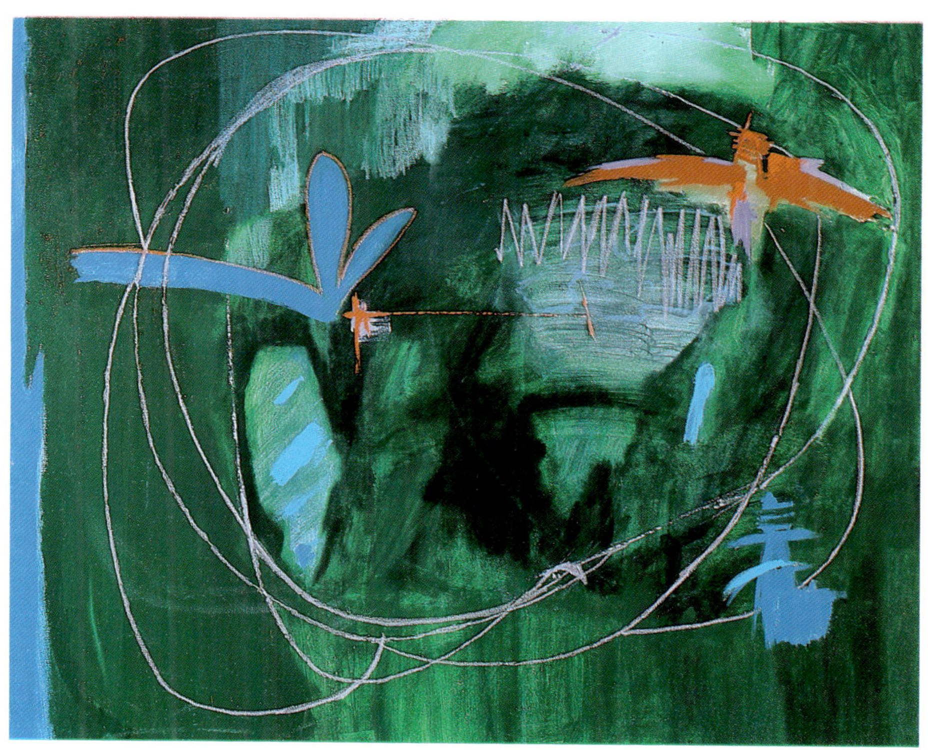

VIRGINIA DEHN

Spirit
Acrylic on canvas
40 x 48 Inches

With my paintings I feel akin to an archaeologist. I am digging into layers of my unconscious. The final image is the result of a search, perhaps connected through time with a forgotten universal knowledge.

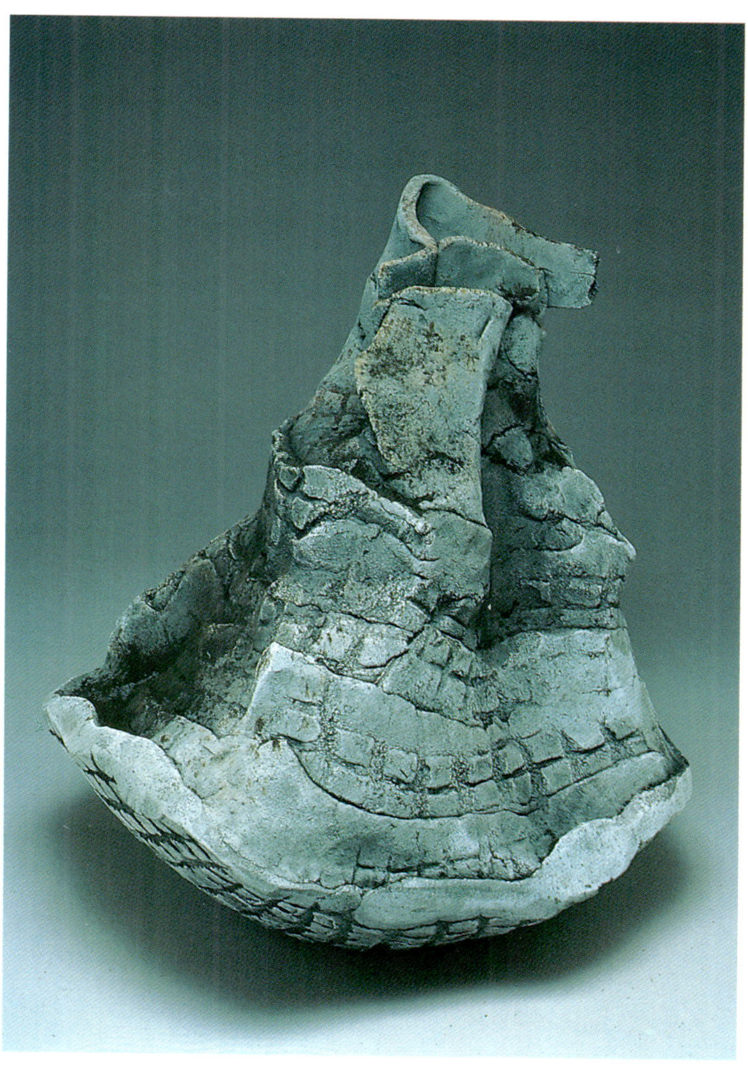

MARY ELLEN DWYER

Eumachia
Sagger fire
14 1/2 x 9 x 8 Inches

As part of the rock I illustrate, I hope to awaken the perspective of the viewer in some way, to nature's ephemeral bounty.

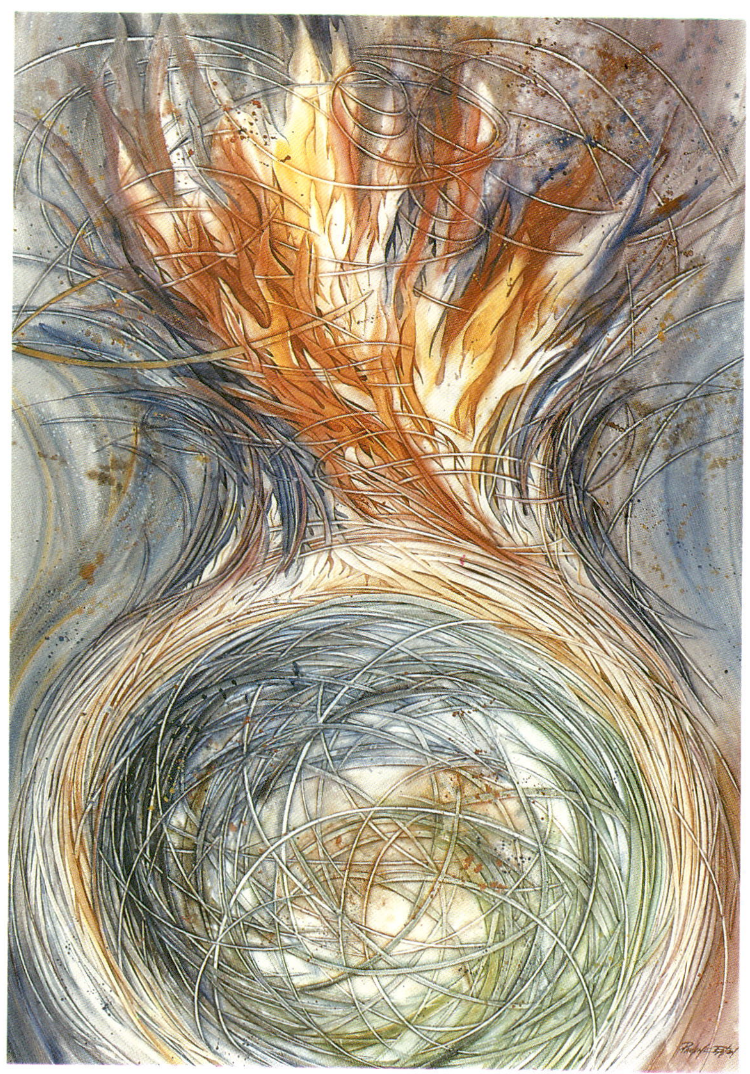

PAULINE EATON

Noosphere Aflame
Watercolor
60 x 40 Inches

"Noosphere Aflame" illuminates Pierre Teillard de Chardin's concept of the envelope of Spirit Energy encircling the planet. I paint into the wedge of meaning between layers of spiritual and material reality.

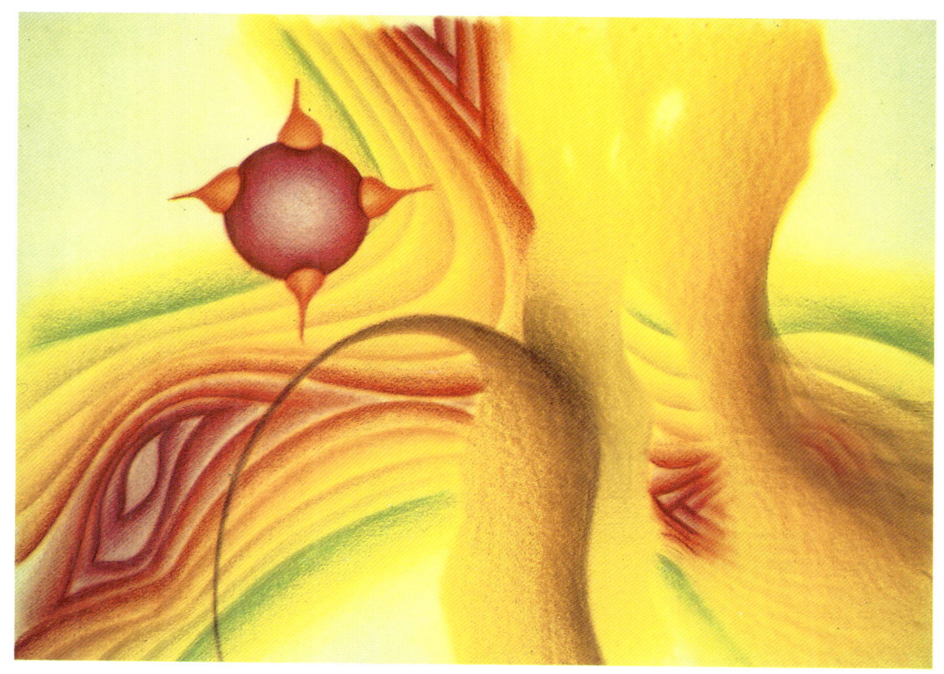

DAVID EHRLICH

A Child's Dream
Film Animation: six layers of drawing
(prismacolor pencil on tracing paper)
underlit and filmed from above
8 1/2 x 11 1/2 Inches

*Underlighting and filming six drawings
simultaneously achieves a saturation of color
and light existing only in dream, and these
animated images transform in layered time,
they gain an anima, gentle and meditative.*

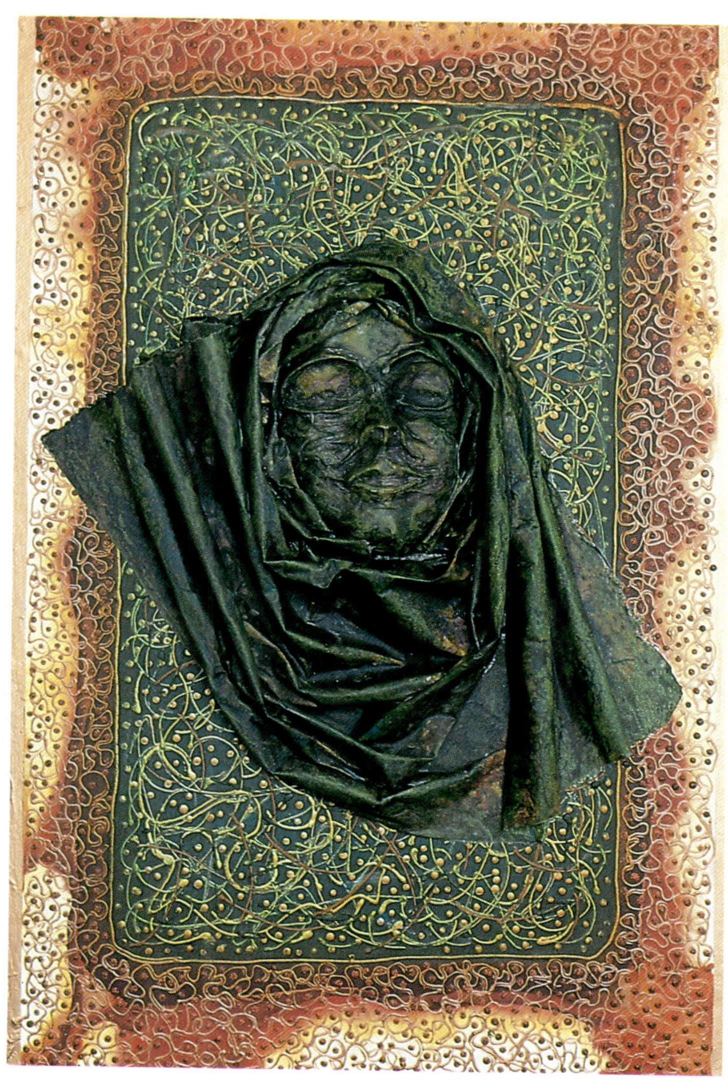

SALLY EMSLIE

Mother of Grace
Mixed media on wood
28 X 18 Inches

*Steeped as I was in my childhood Catholicism,
I built many grotts to the Blessed Mother, hoping
she would appear - and one day I believe she
did. Her image remains in my mind.*

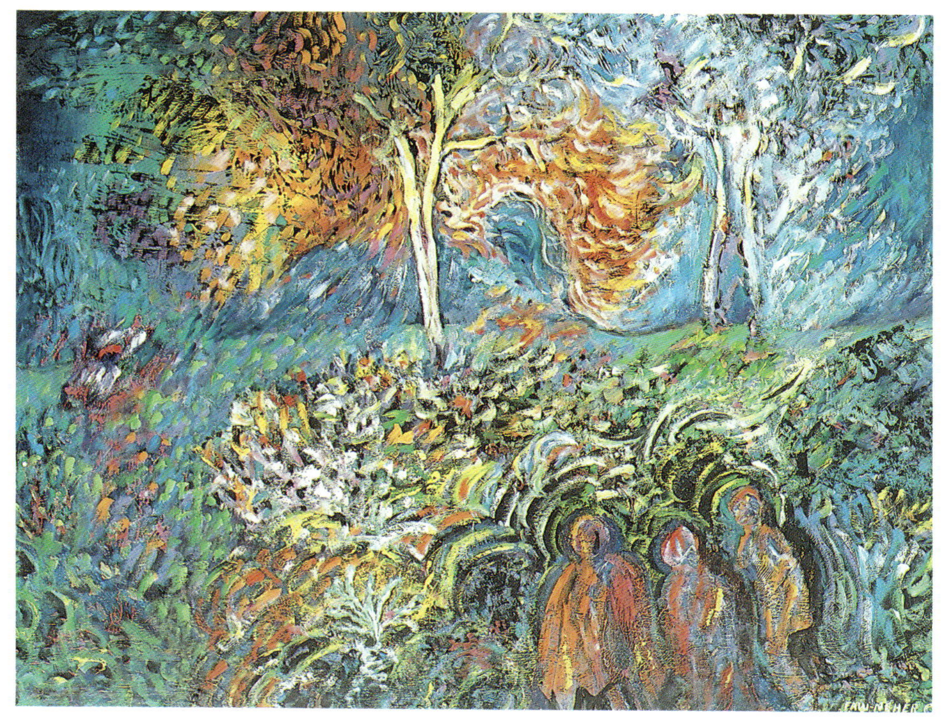

LINDA FAW-NEHER

Light Ceremony
Acrylic on museum board
40 x 32 Inches

*This painting emerged as if I had seen it before,
either in a dream, a vision or just as an idea
floating around in my head, waiting to be born.*

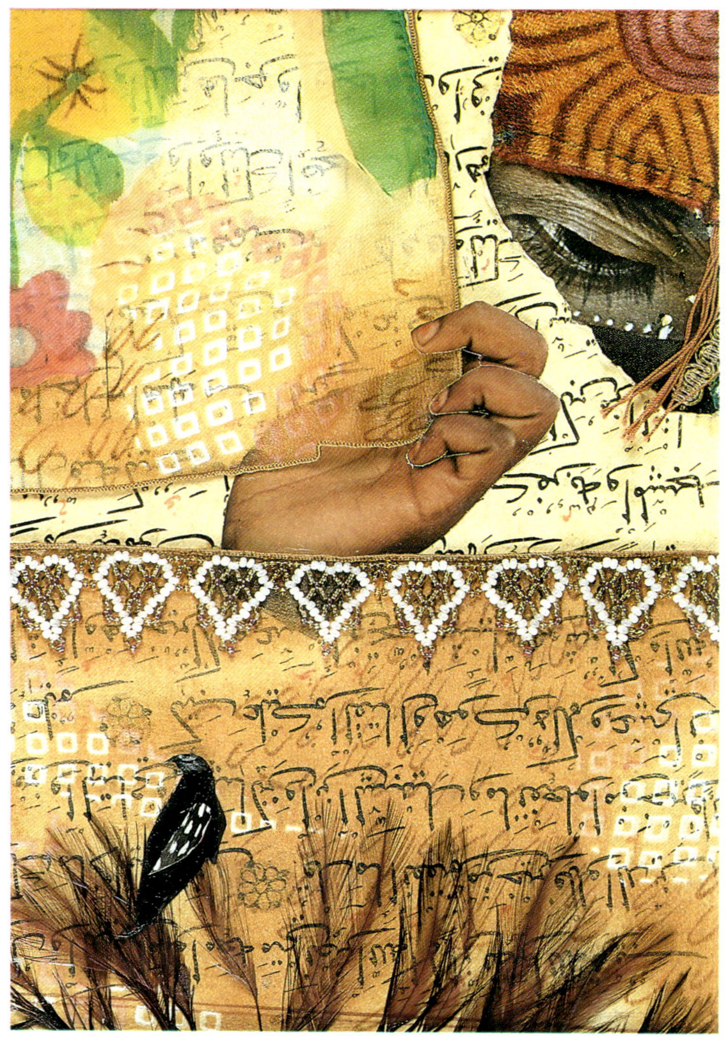

BEVERLY GOLDSMAN

Veiled Illusion
Mixed media
11 x 15 Inches

We veil ourselves in many ways. My recent work employs veiling to remind me that behind each veil exists a human being looking out and, sometimes, seeking contact.

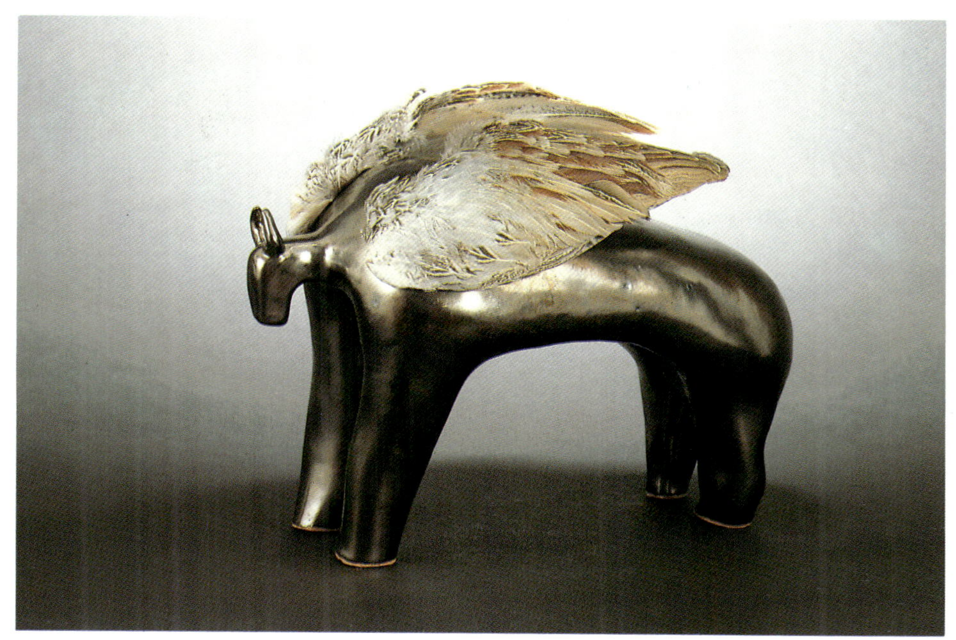

ILENA GRAYSON

Golden Dust of Sunset
Earthenware clay with bronze glaze
9 x 12 x 6 Inches

I personally seek to explore and interpret ancient cultures along with nature's simplicity. The organic shapes and tactile elements reflect the influence of vegetation and geological formations.

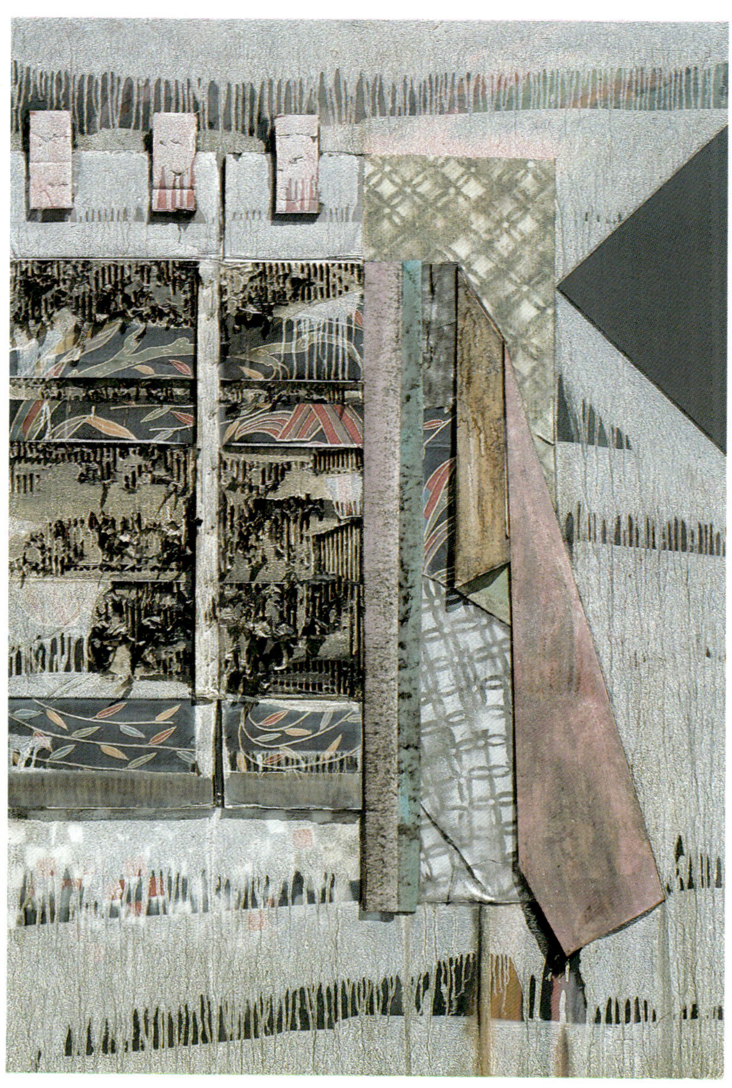

STANLEY G. GROSSE

Kinki Nippon Series - Toji- The Sale
Mixed media on canvas
60 x 40 Inches

*I consider my paintings to be mixed media collage.
In these Japanese influenced abstractions I use
a layering process to recreate aged patinas, soft
textures and subtle colorations.*

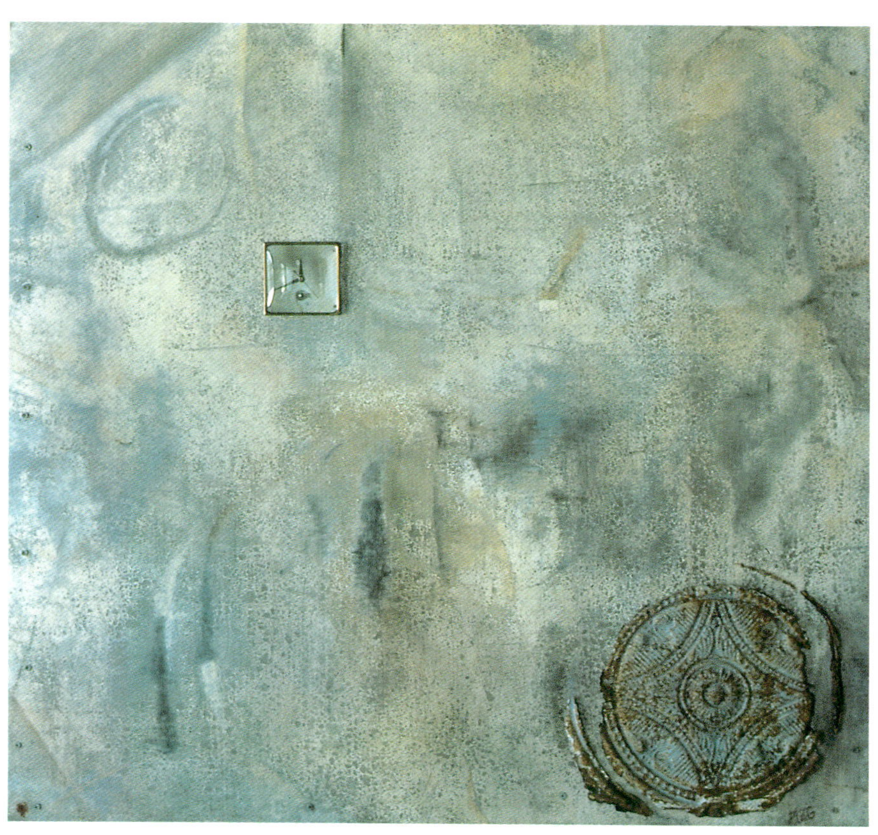

MARLENE ZANDER GUTIERREZ

"The Eighth Day" View I
(one of three views from a series on
The Redemption of Matter)
Distressed tin, acrylic and collage
43 x 43 1/2 X 2 Inches

*With ugly, discarded tin, I wanted to manifest
whatever beauty could be created by burning,
by re-interpreting nail holes and wrinkles with
subtle paint layers and a few symbolic attached
items.*

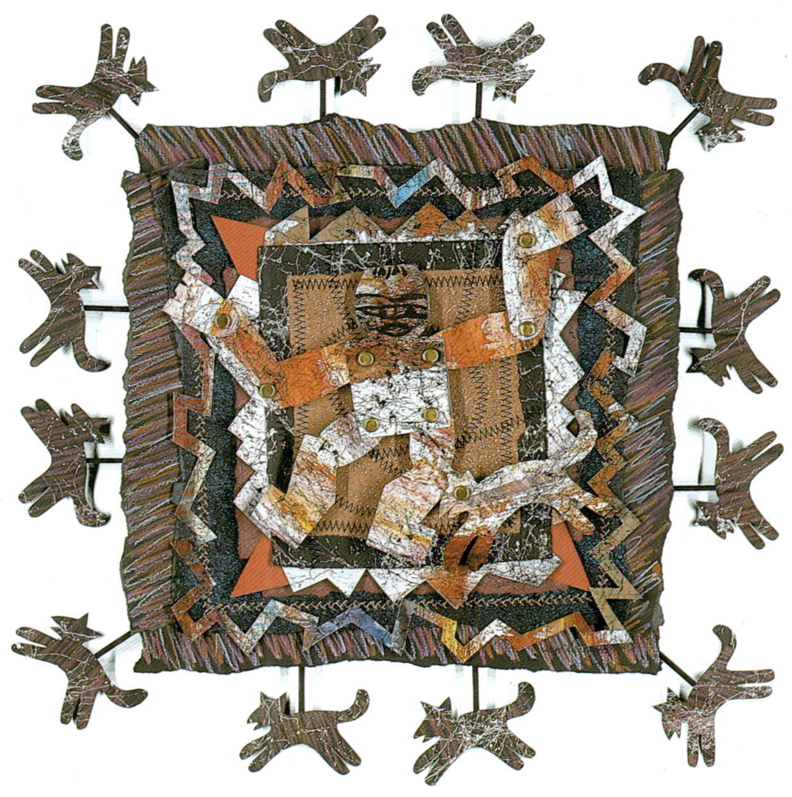

ANN L. HARTLEY

See Man Dance
Mixed media
21 x 21 Inches

See man dance....see wolf run.
Universal man dances while world burns,
wolf runs to warn man they are both endangered.

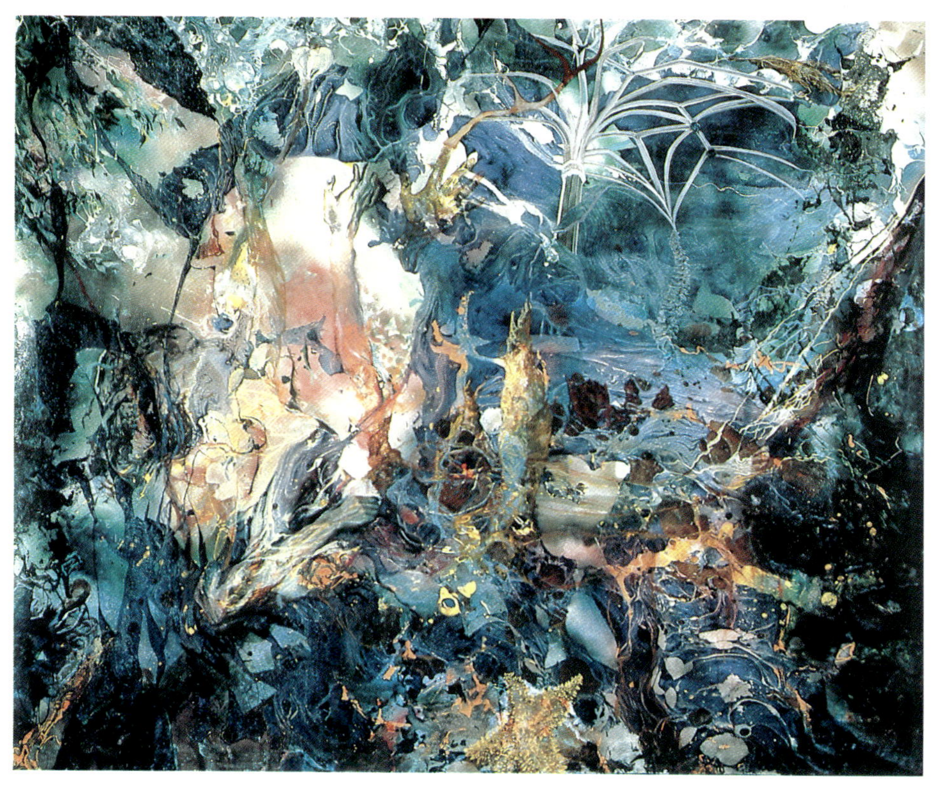

MARY F. HUGHES

Reaching
Oil and acrylic
60 x 72 Inches

*Layered and marbled patterns form a miniature
cosmic landscape, a record of cosmic order
from thought to matter. Metaphorically mirroring
psychological thoughts, feelings, and symbols
that form the structure of human development.*

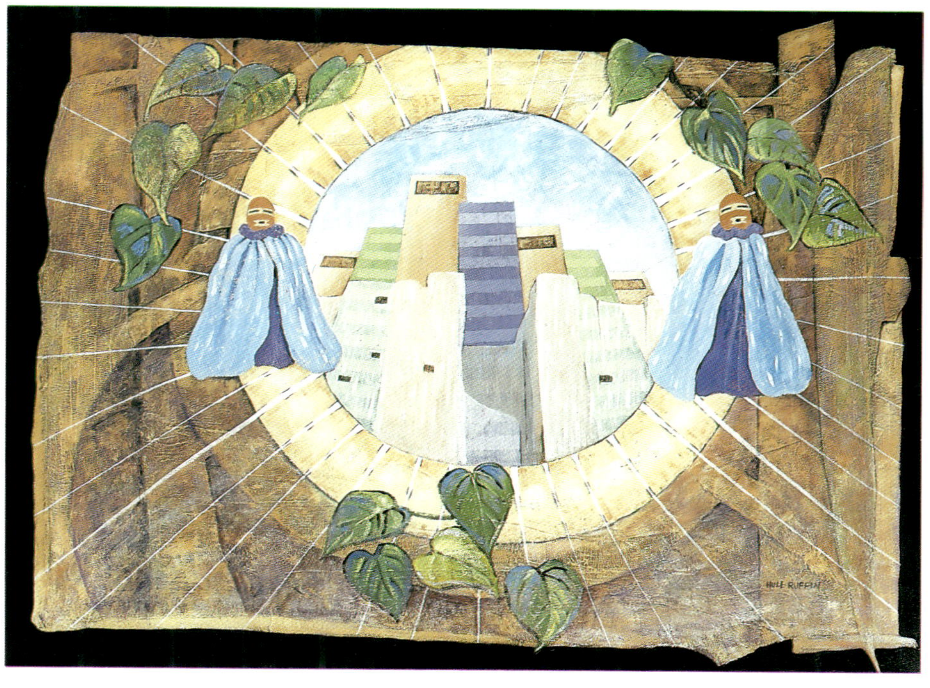

JANET HULL-RUFFIN

First Mesa
Acrylic
36 x 48 Inches

I have always used art as a way of revealing and healing the many parts of myself. Now I am using art as a way of healing earth life.

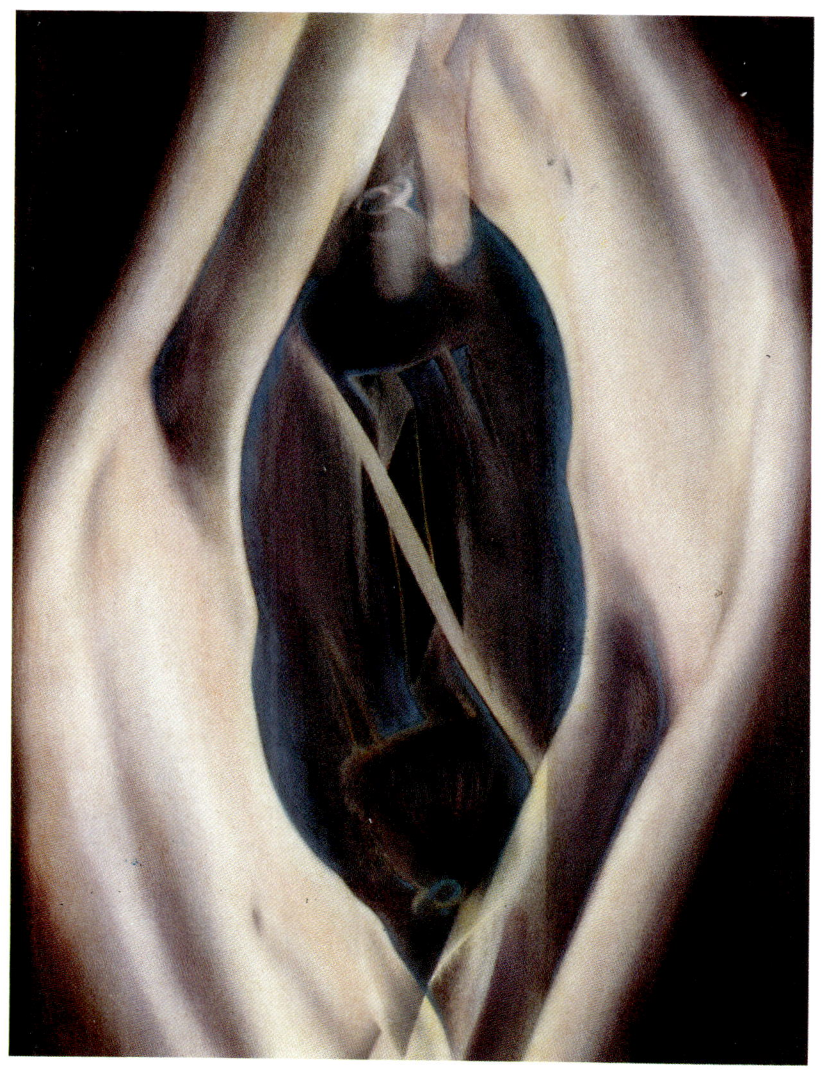

LAURI DICKINSON JACK

Emanations I
Manipulated, painted photograph
25 x 20 Inches

My images evolve from the intuitive processing of layers of experience, memories and dreams. A journey that is filled with mysteries and hidden messages. Layering is inherent, complex and the path to truth.

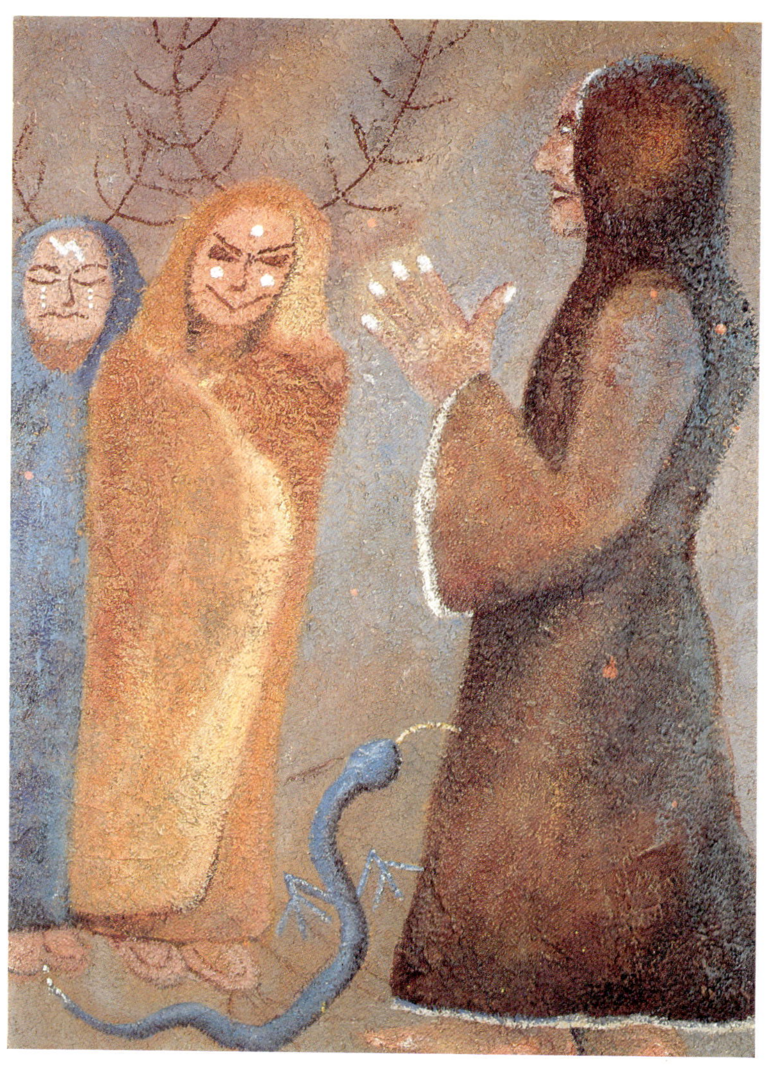

JUNE F. JOHNSTON

Shaman
Acrylic, mixed media
48 x 36 Inches

This work is from the series "Ancient Origins" which is derived from cane and rock art. The religious symbolism represents the Shaman of ancient religions and the Christian figure of Western Culture.

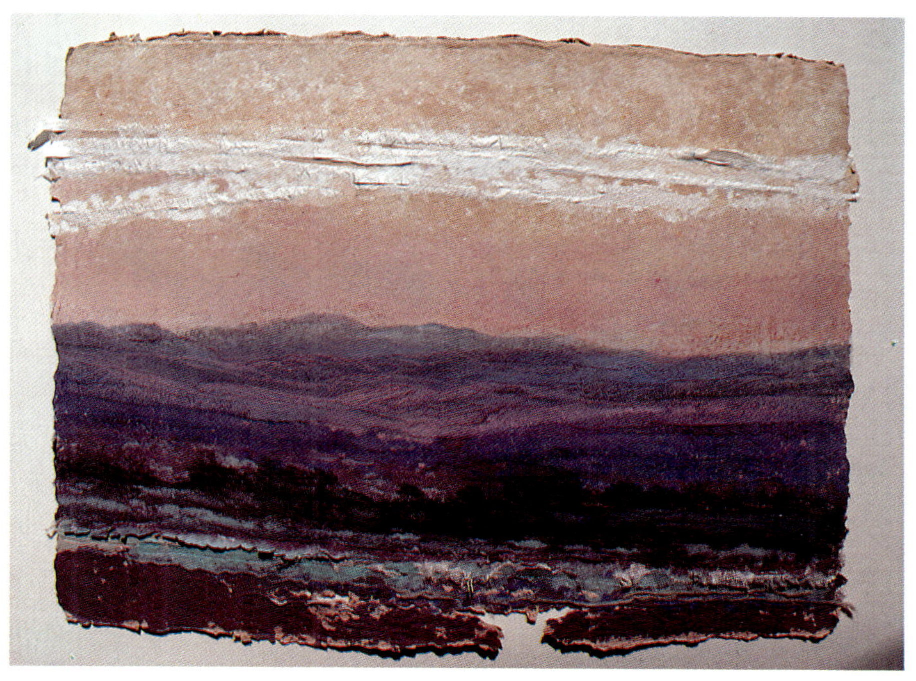

NORMA L. JONES

Strata
Mixed media on handmade paper
30 x 40 Inches

*To me, paintings need to express a mood,
a feeling. I like to build up many layers of
color in order to see translucent areas
creating a feeling of mystery...of time.*

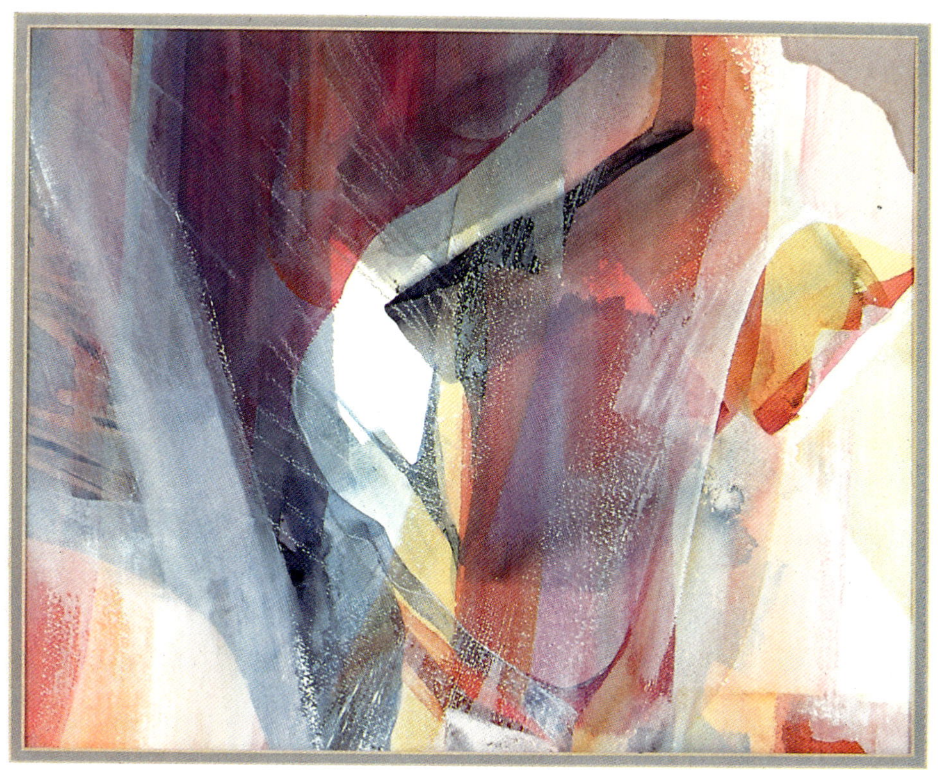

BETTY D. KEISEL

Transformation
Watermedia
16 x 19 Inches

*My work is an integral part of my life
in which I can express my feelings and
concepts of existence.*

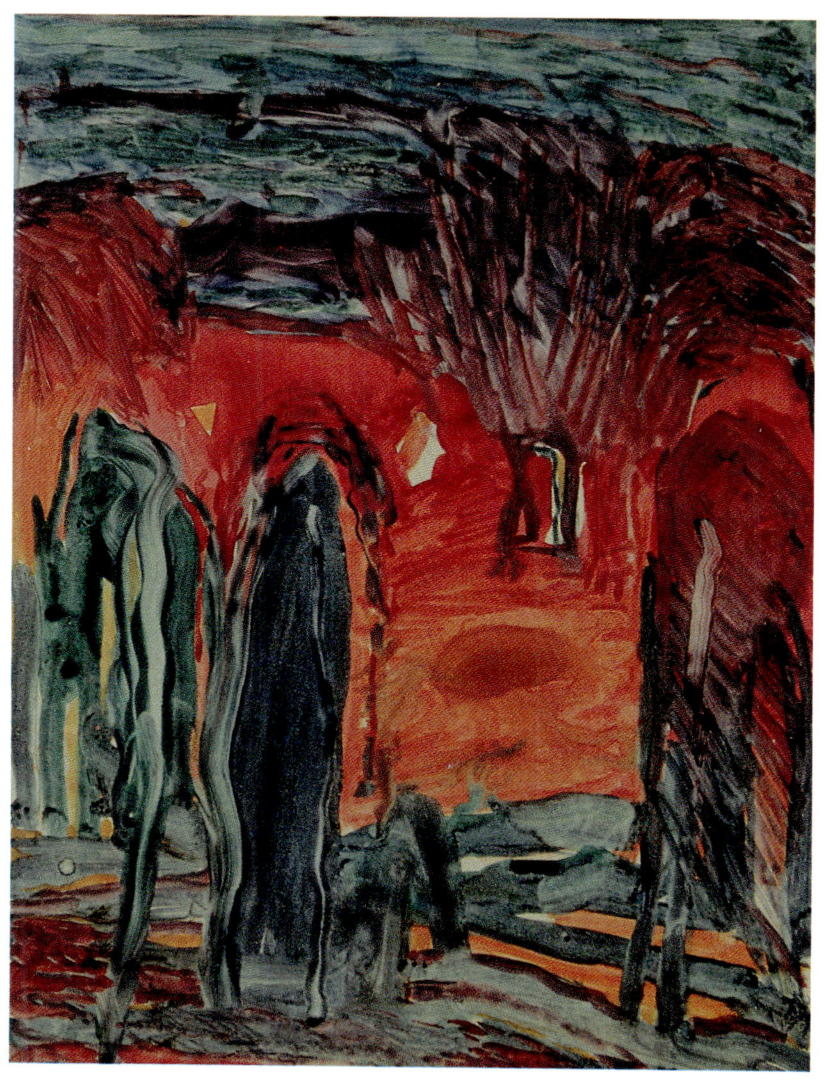

KATHLEEN KUCHAR

Desert Walk
Watercolor monotype
15 1/2 x 11 1/2 Inches

*My work exists and does not represent any
one thing in nature. It has a life of its own.*

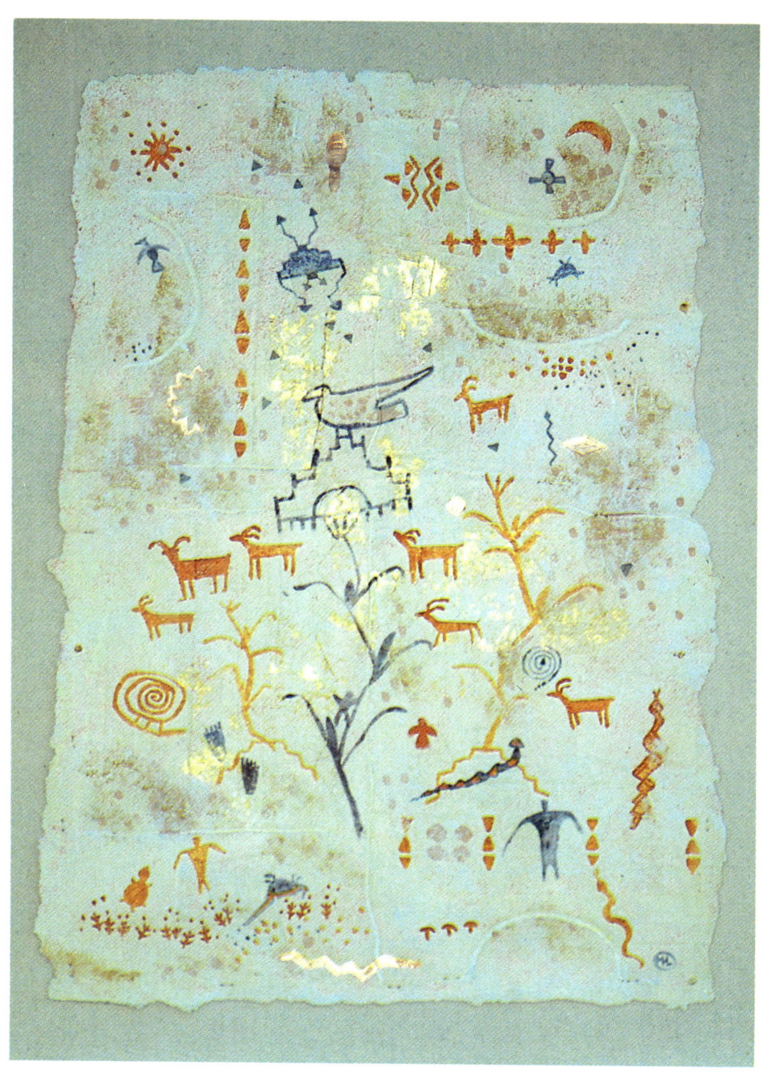

MARY LANGSTON

Harvest
Mixed media on handmade paper
40 x 28 Inches

Layering materials is an exciting process for me, relating to an awareness of nature's cycles as well as a bond with the myths and rituals of all time.

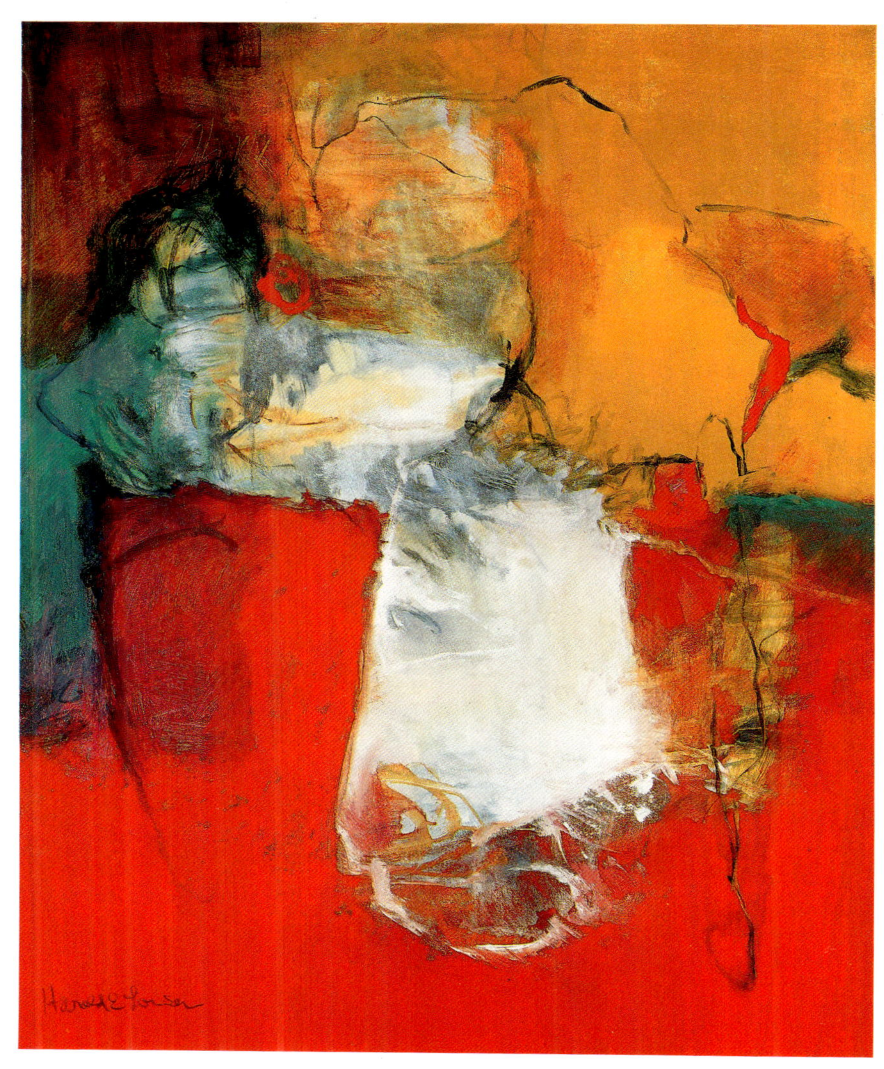

HAROLD E. LARSEN

Dreaming
Acrylic on canvas
32 x 40 Inches

*I find that one of the constants in my life is
putting marks on paper and canvas.
These marks come from the inner me
and are not tied to what I perceive as the
world outside me.*

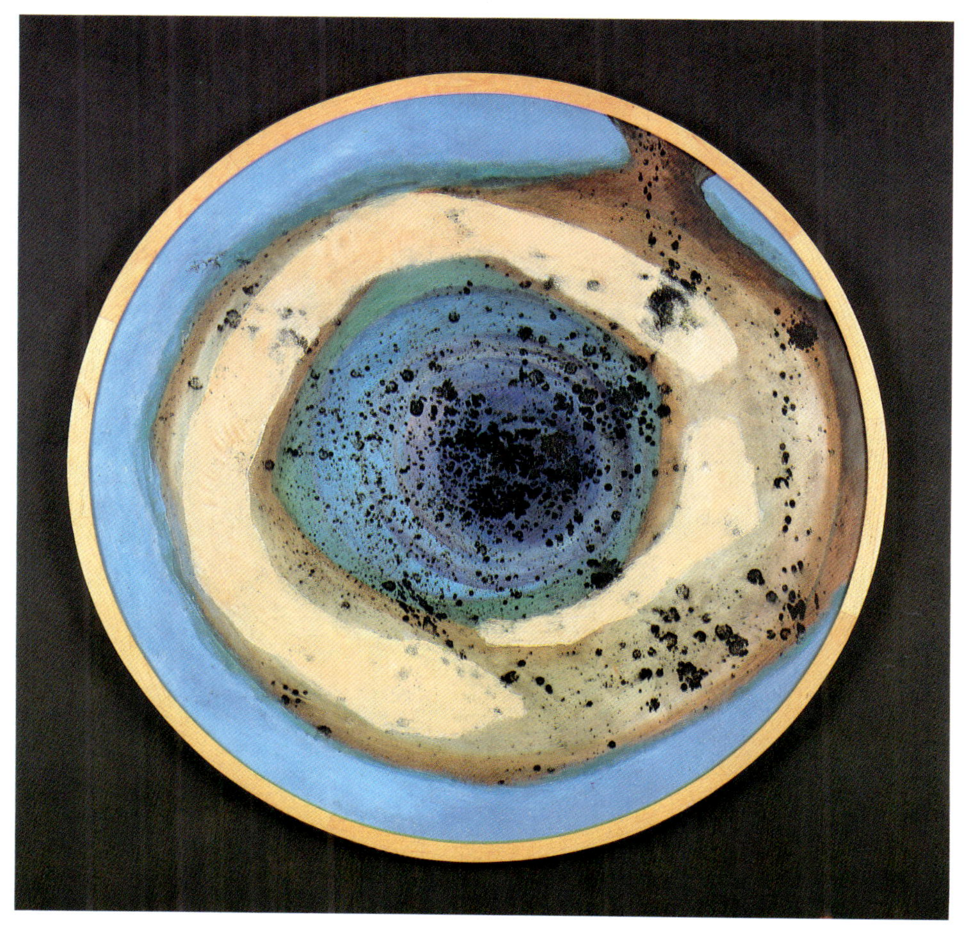

INGRID LEEDS

Geozone I
Acrylic and ink on canvas
26 Inches tondo

My Geozone Series is abstractions of earth's cycles in time and space. From the moon, earth's colors glow radiantly; let's weave a patch for the ozone layer, our cosmic shield.

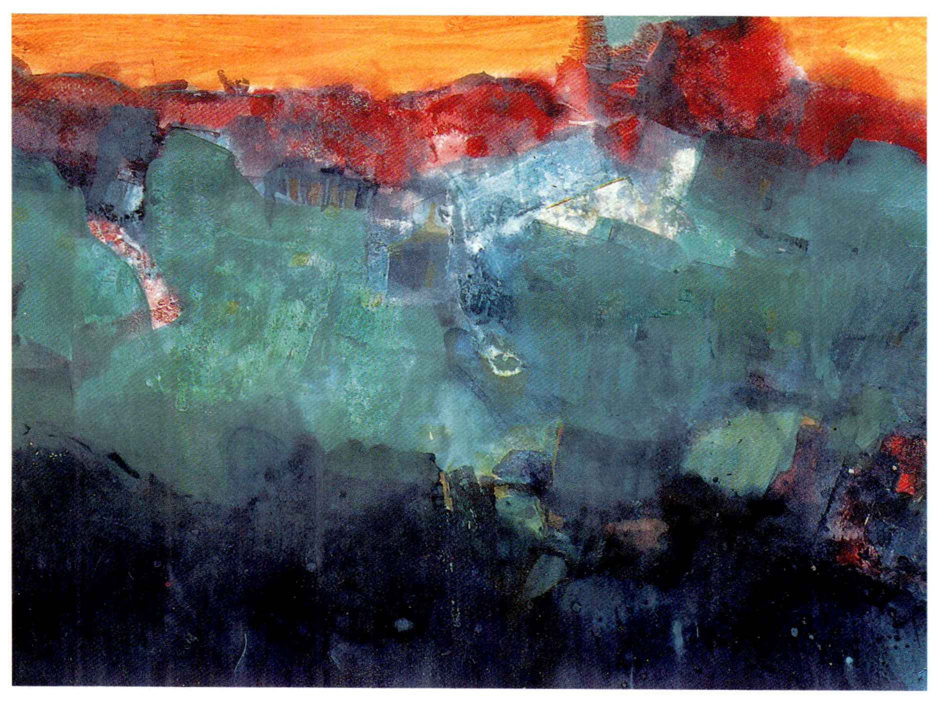

MARIE DOLMAS LEKORENOS

Sunset
Acrylic
30 x 22 1/2 Inches

Sunset, when the brilliant sky touches the dark earth, signals the edge of night, the beginning of rest, a renewal of my inner spirit.

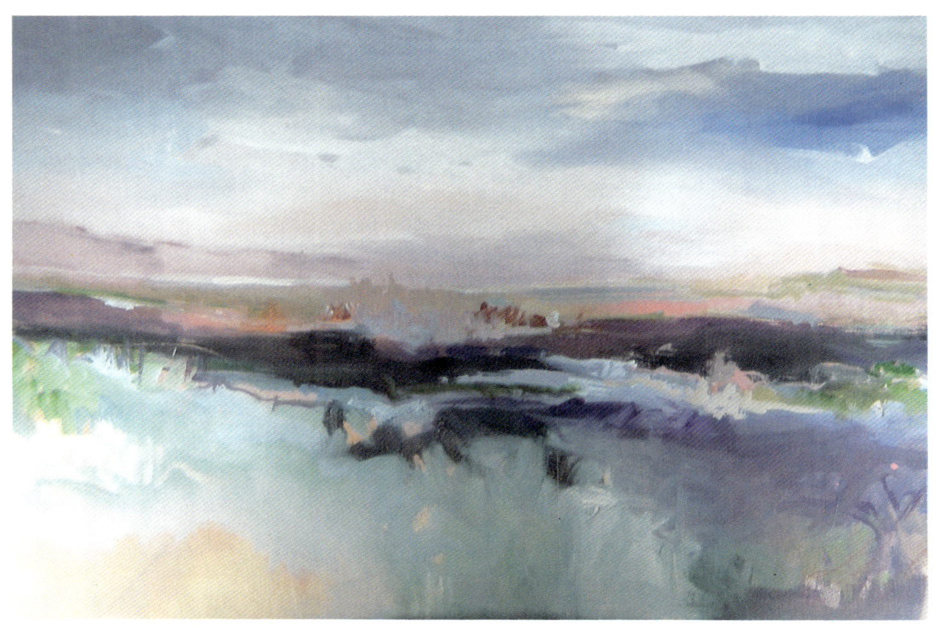

MARLENE LENKER

Spirit of Manitou
Acrylic, gouache and pastel on paper
30 x 42 Inches

*Layers of color, transparent and opaque
are used to create a mood, a feeling of
place and space. The layers permit
enhancement by exposing fragments and
markings, expressing my inner journey.*

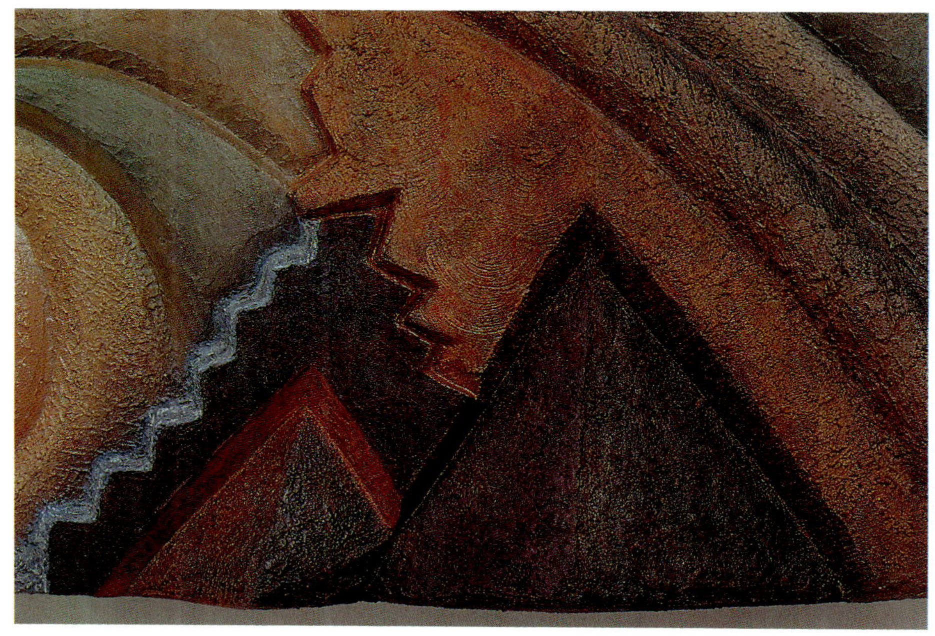

LYNDA LEONARD

Looking Through the Veil of the Continuum
Mixed media
17 x 37 x 4 Inches
(Detail)

*Through the universal language of geometry
I create work that reflects our history/future,
the mystery and magic of life. Works about
places in the heart and mind, spaces in time.*

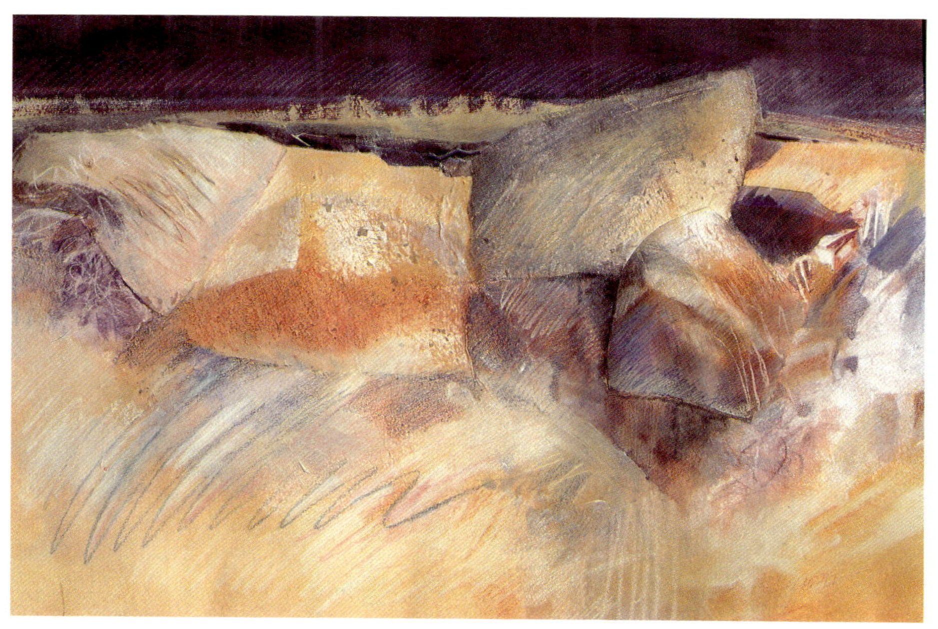

MARTA LIGHT

Desert Reach
Mixed media
11 x 18 Inches

*The power and presence of the land
both draws and pushes me away...
healing, and finally containing me.*

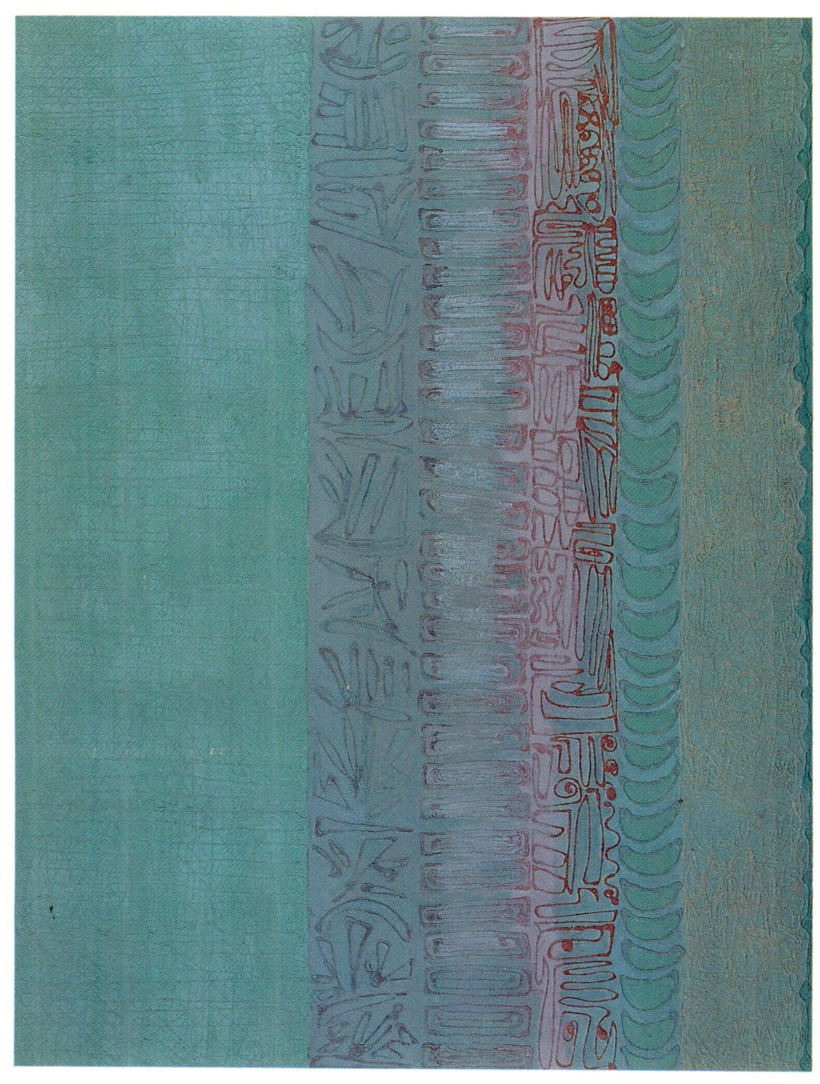

MARILYN MARKOWITZ

Origins 002
Acrylic and sand on canvas
66 x 88 Inches

*Outside forces are absorbed and
integrated into an artist's being. They are
brought forth, layer by layer, to finalize
into a new creative entity.*

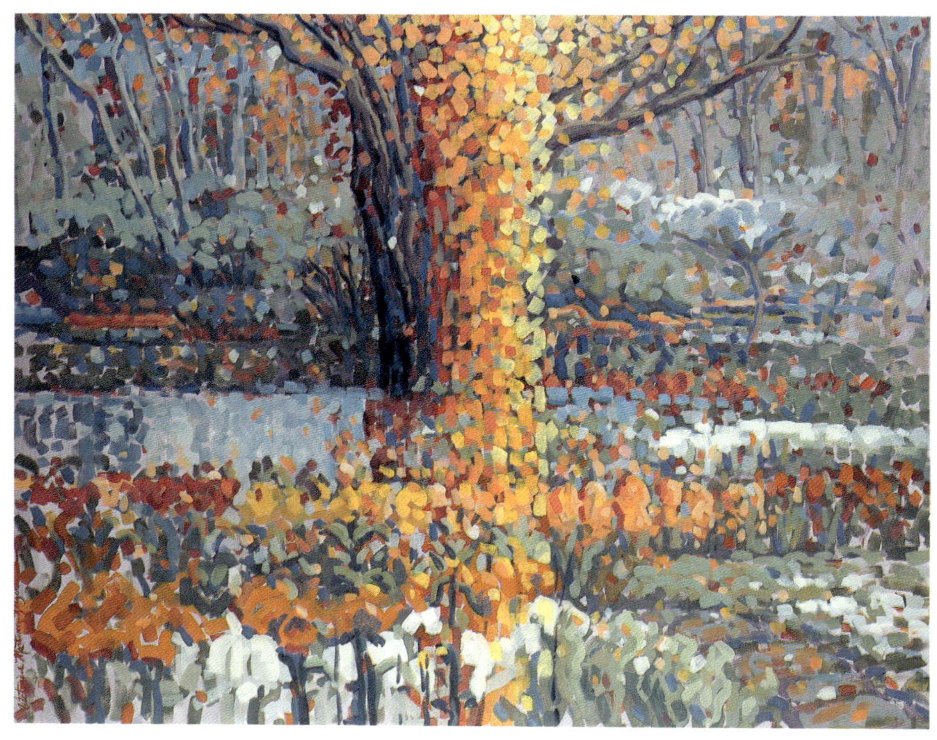

VICTORIA MARTINEZ-RODGERS

Divine Healer-Millennium Series
Oil
48 x 60 Inches

*The Grail is a miraculous vessel filled with
the fire and light of the Divine. It possesses
the power to heal on all levels and inspires
strength and wisdom.*

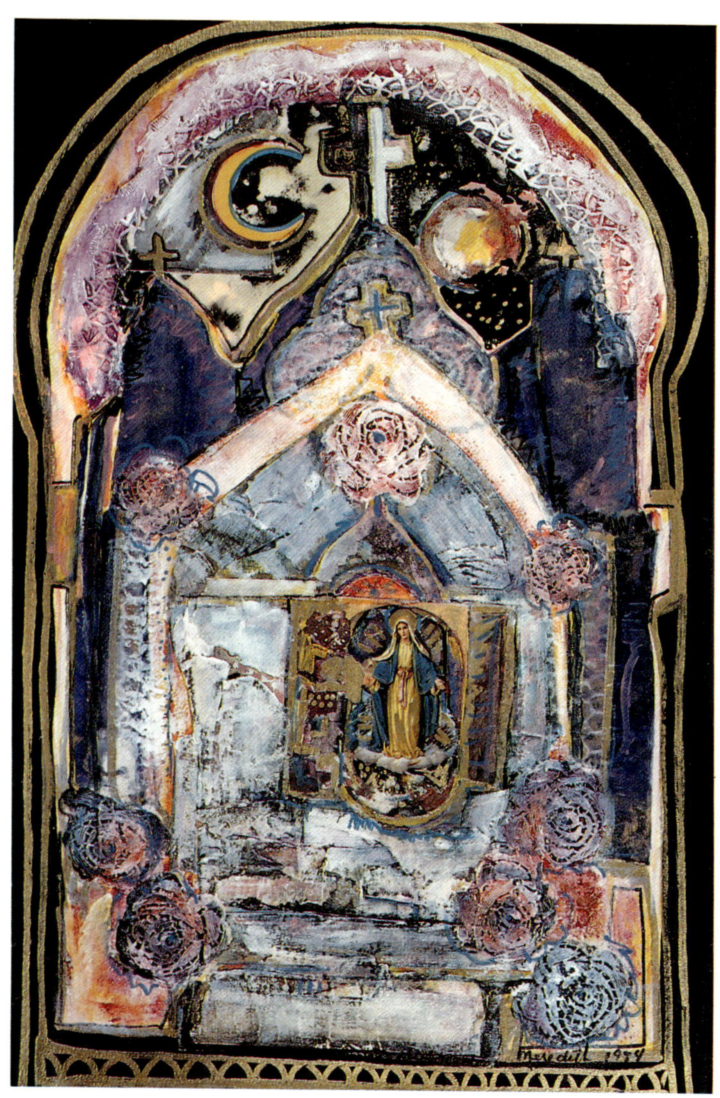

RUTH MEREDITH

Shrines IV

Collage and acrylic on paper
19 1/2 x 12 1/4 Inches

I create symbolic forms woven from the reality of my own life. Emerging from the fluid boundary between order and chaos, forms and concepts dissolve and re-emerge transformed, reflecting their source in the sacred.

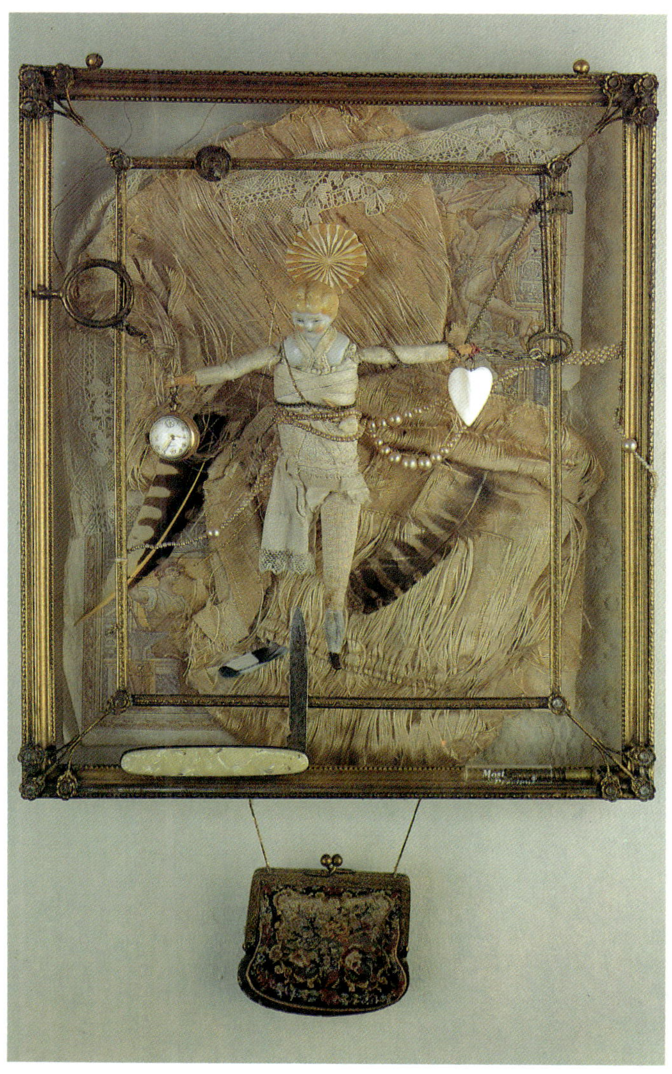

ELAINE WALLACE MORRIS

Most Precious
Assemblage
10 X 14 X 3 Inches

I recycle myself, placing objects from my past in environments which clarify the present. Constantly changing ideas and emotions are glued, hammered and stitched into the uneasy balance of my art.

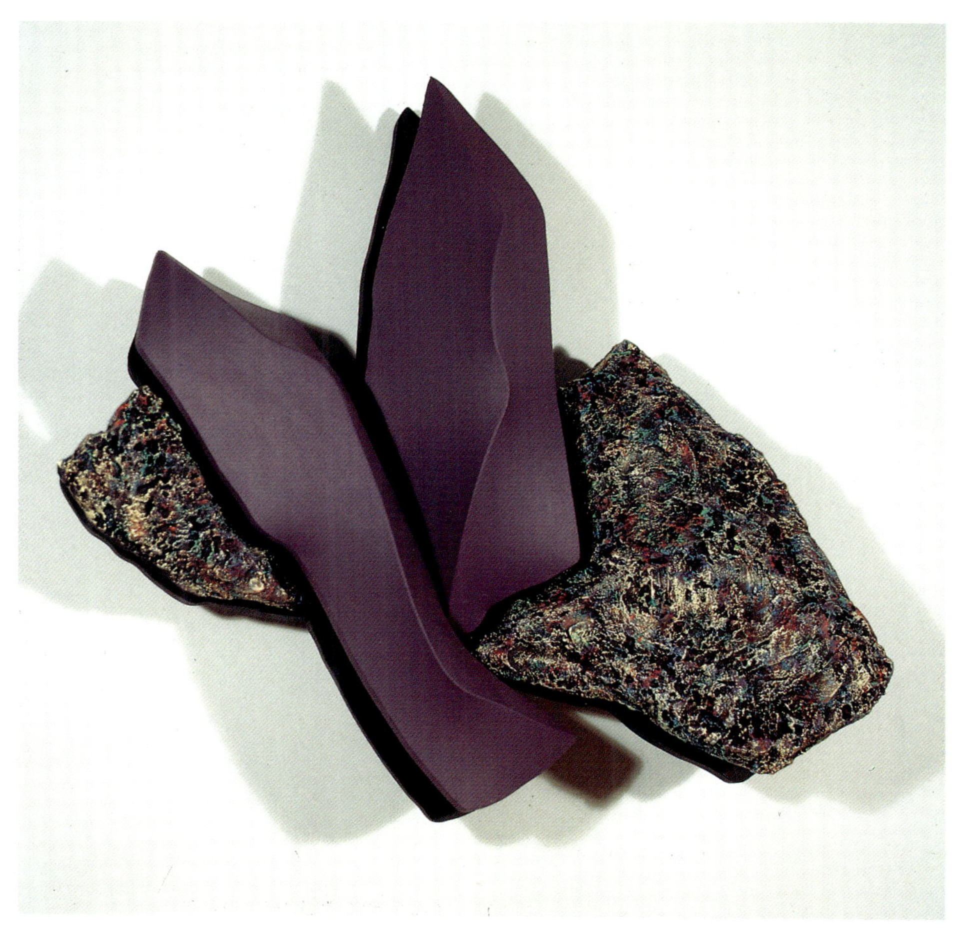

PAT MUSICK

Epilogue 15
Mixed media
37 x 38 x 12 Inches

I form my constructions in ways which provide varying levels of permanence through change, continuity through movement, constant transformation, and complex, elastic, infinitely varying perceptions.

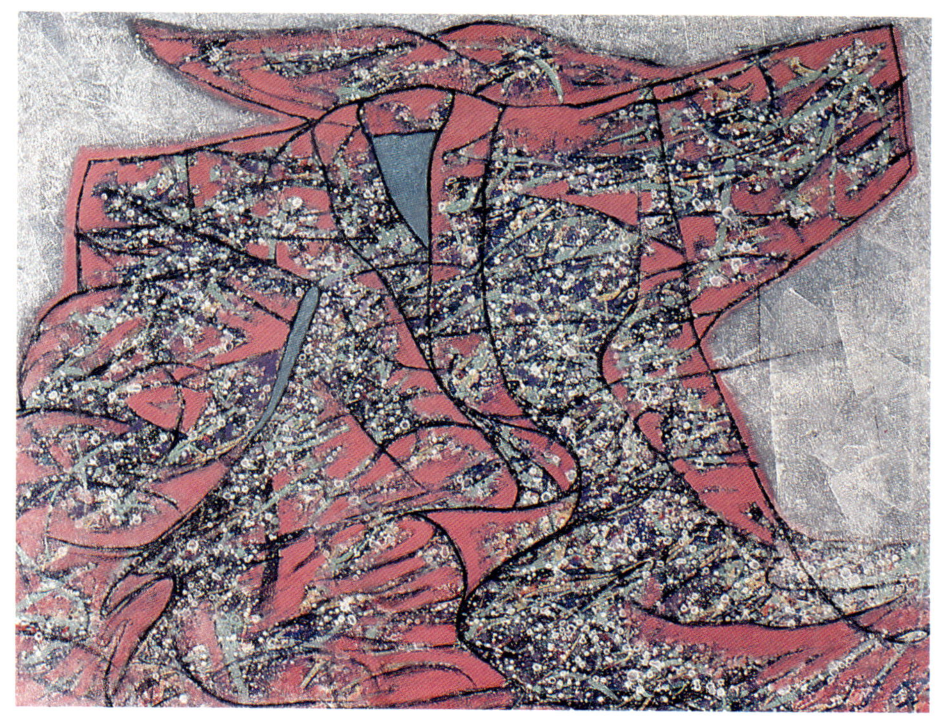

IKU NAGAI

Celebration for Women I
Watermedia and mineral pigments on paper
38 x 48 Inches

"Celebration for Women" is a symbolic representation of women's roles in the family and society. The kimono is a symbol of festivity and a metaphor to acknowledge women's rights to celebrate her achievements and creativity.

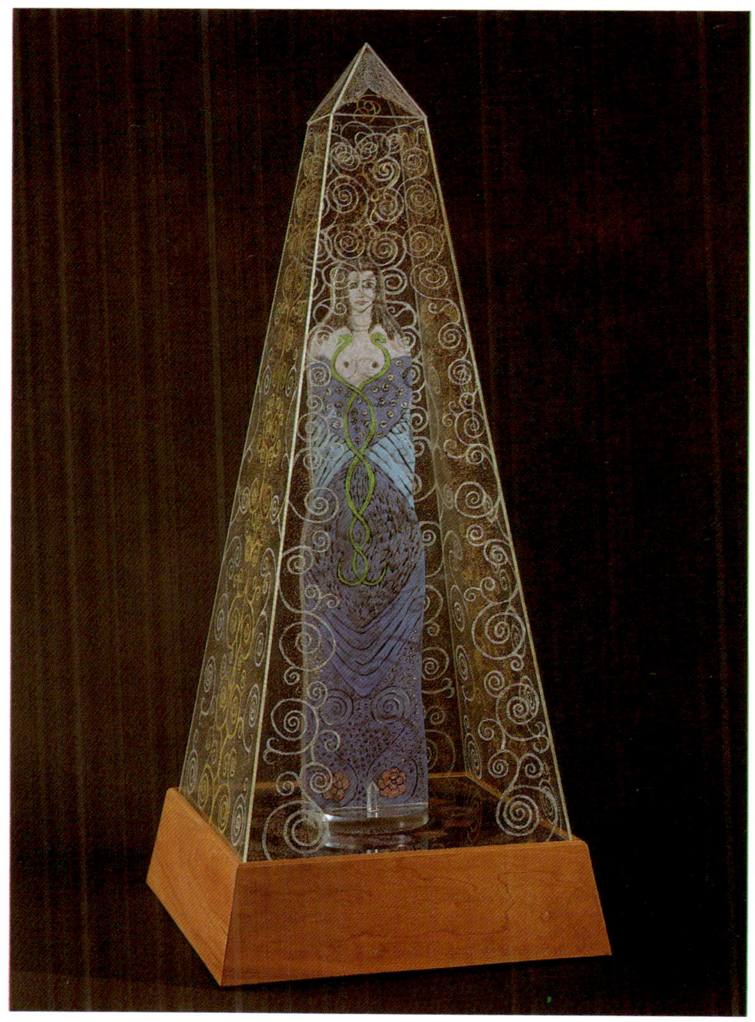

MARY CARROLL NELSON

Shrine to Sophia

Plexiglass, gold leaf, ink, wood, light and
crystals
57 x 23 x 23 Inches

*Sophia, Goddess of Wisdom, through the inner
shadow, teaches.
From light and dark, the dove, the serpent and
the rose, she reaches.*

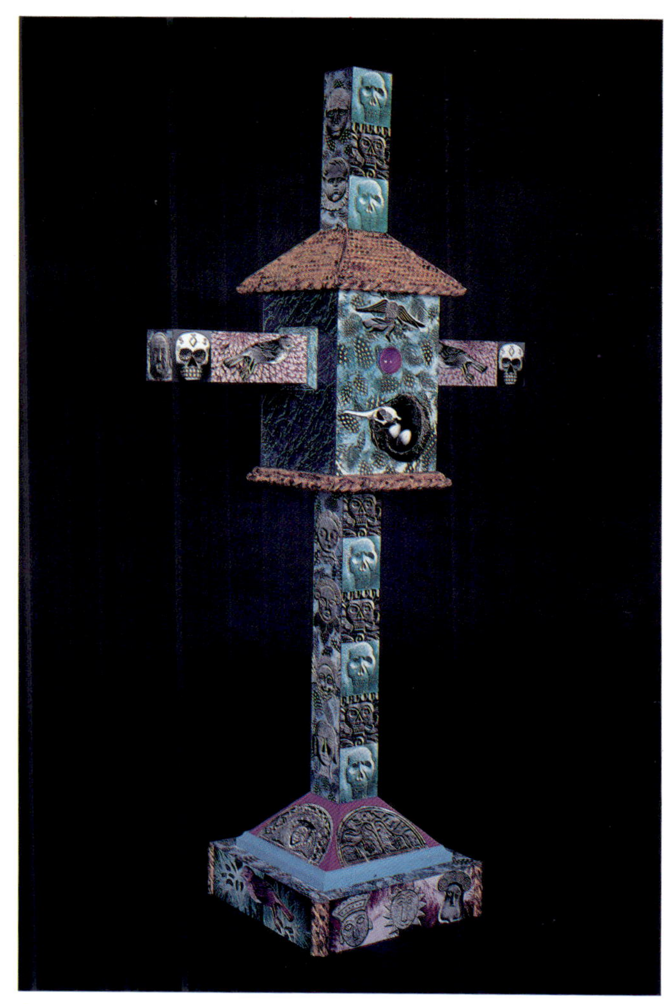

RICHARD NEWMAN

Bird Soul Catcher Monument
Mixed media sculpture
56 x 28 x 13 Inches

My work attempts to interrelate experience and bridge time by letting the past inform the present. Fragments are assembled to create a new construct of meaning. Diverse thoughts and feelings are connected; polar forces and energies are brought into balance.

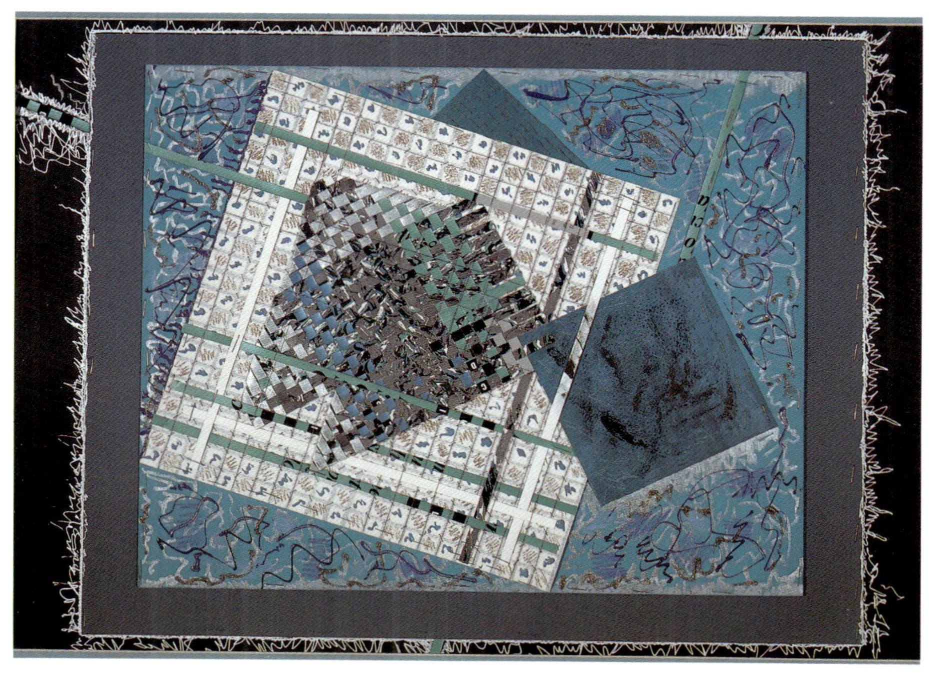

ROCHELLE NEWMAN

Maverick Moment #2
Mixed Media: woven elements, thread, acrylic,
paper
24 x 30 Inches

SIX BY FIVE = 30 WORDS   THE PLIABLE PLANE SURFACE
fiber • paper • manipulated • bounded • visible
tactile • universal • abstract • rational • expressive
metaphoric • vibrant • personal • powerful • truthful
symmetric/asymmetric • asymmetric/symmetric structures

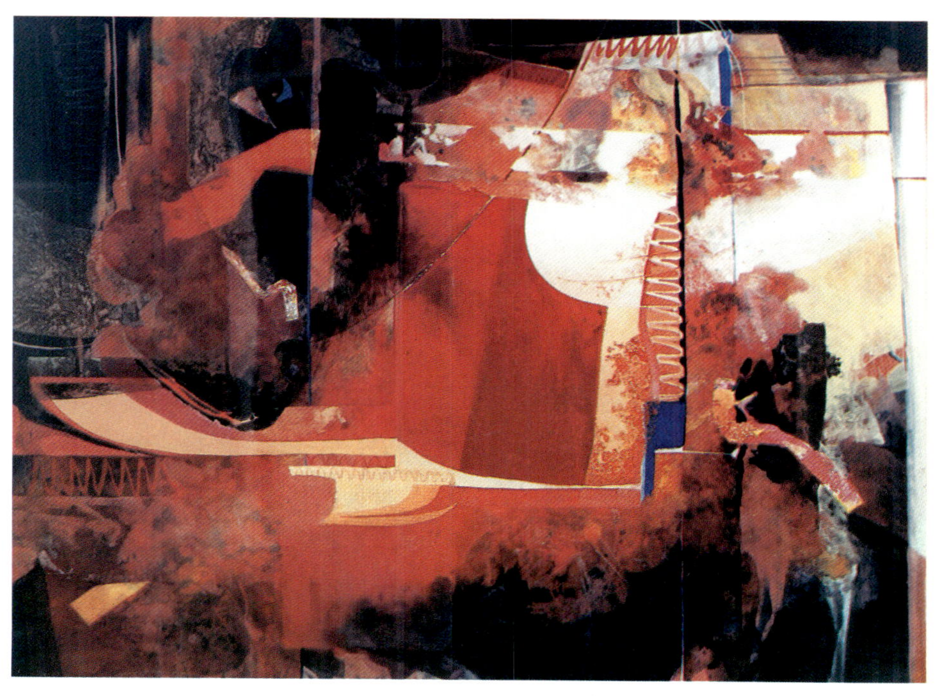

MARILYN HUGHEY PHILLIS

Labyrinths and Distillations
Acrylic and rice paper collage
30 x 40 Inches

*The complexity and mystery of the organic,
geological and energy processes of the earth
have always intrigued me and filled me with
unending reverence toward our planet.*

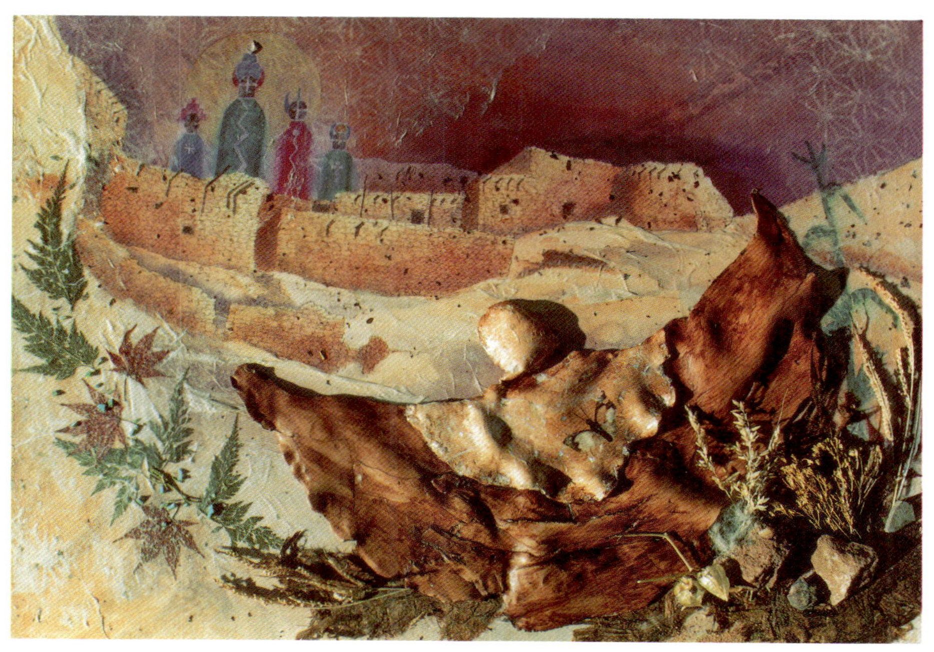

CYNTHIA PLOSKI

"Mother Earth, Father Sky"

(Three Turkey Ruin, Canyon de Chelly)
Mixed media
22 x 30 Inches

*Mother Earth and Father Sky dance creation.
His seminal energy and her manifesting
energy combine to bring forth the 3-dimensional
world of our existence.*

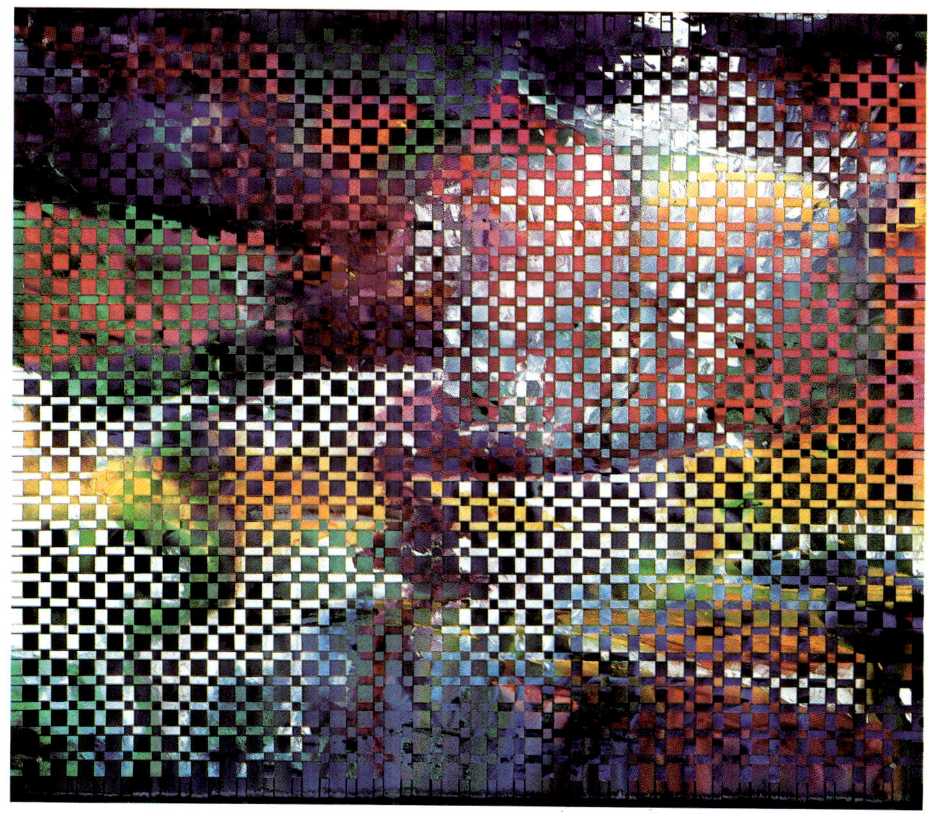

T. F. PODUSKA

Koi

Acrylic on paper
52 x 58 Inches

*A unique order and depth of relationship
is created by my actual weaving process.
The mythical unseen portion emphasizes
the overlapping of time and unspoken
consciousness merging with the visual.*

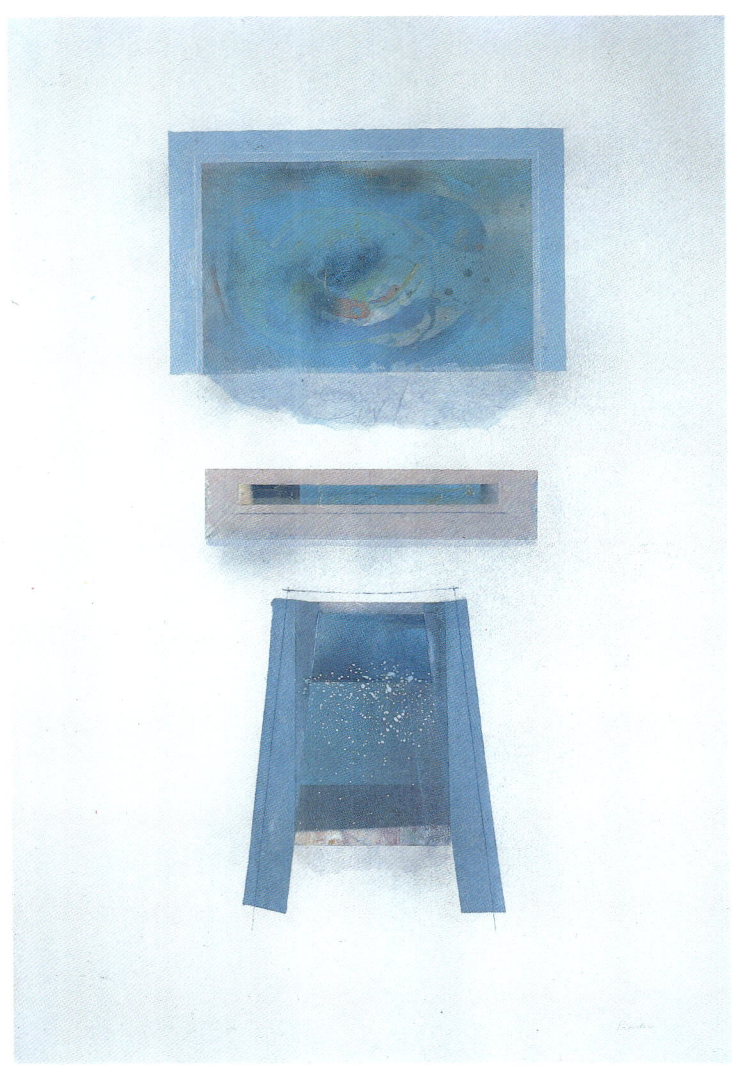

CARL PROVDER

Inner Energy VIII
Mixed media
60 x 40 Inches

Painting is a life adventure without a planned structure. Only by giving into it do I obtain the desired state of tranquility and emptiness to create a vision.

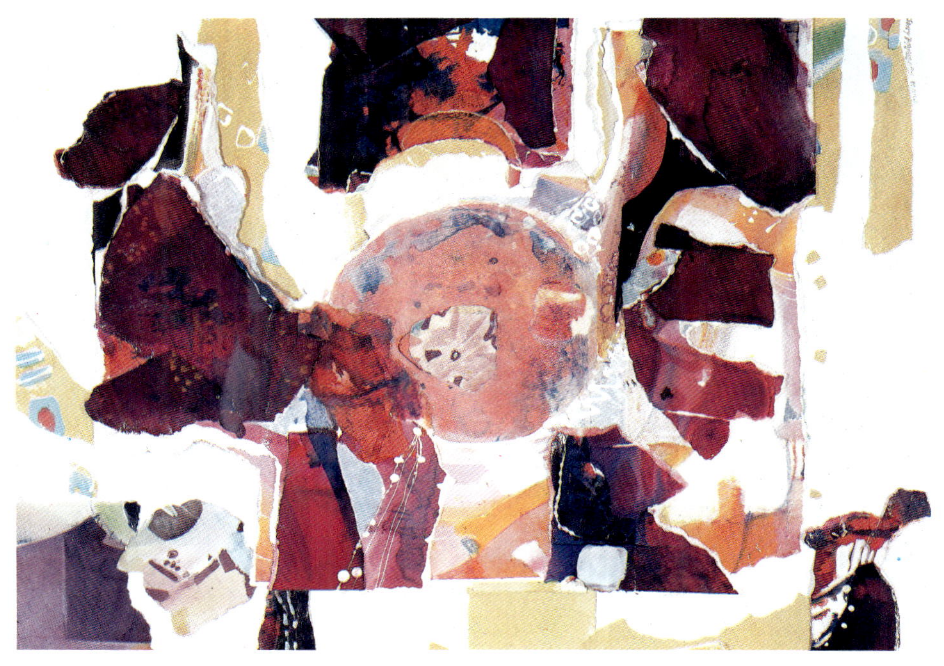

JENY REYNOLDS

Space Involvement
Mixed media
22 x 30 Inches

In the process of inventiveness and connecting color and shapes of various sizes a creative process of our inner images occurs when the mind and body are in tune with one another.

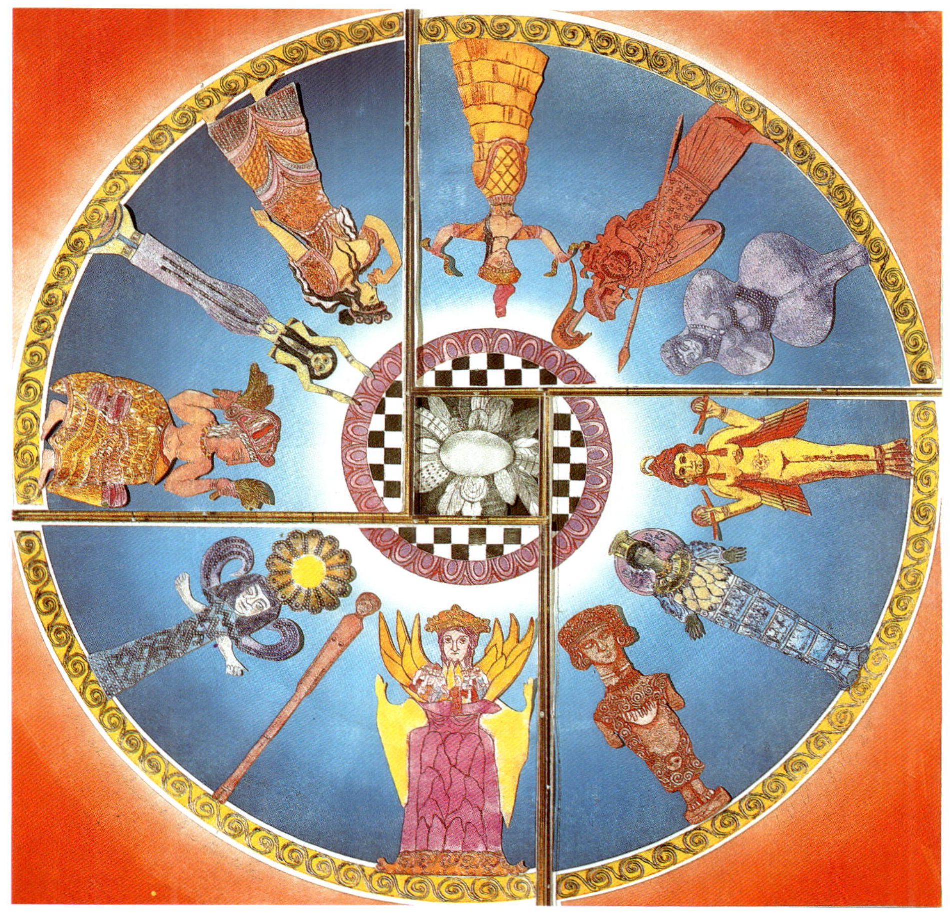

LYDIA RUYLE

The Goddess Has A Thousand Faces
Mandala
Collagraph collage with etching
54 x 54 Inches

I make prints based on inherited images of women from many cultures of the world in order to tell "her stories" of creation, power, life, death, transformation, compassion, beauty, love.

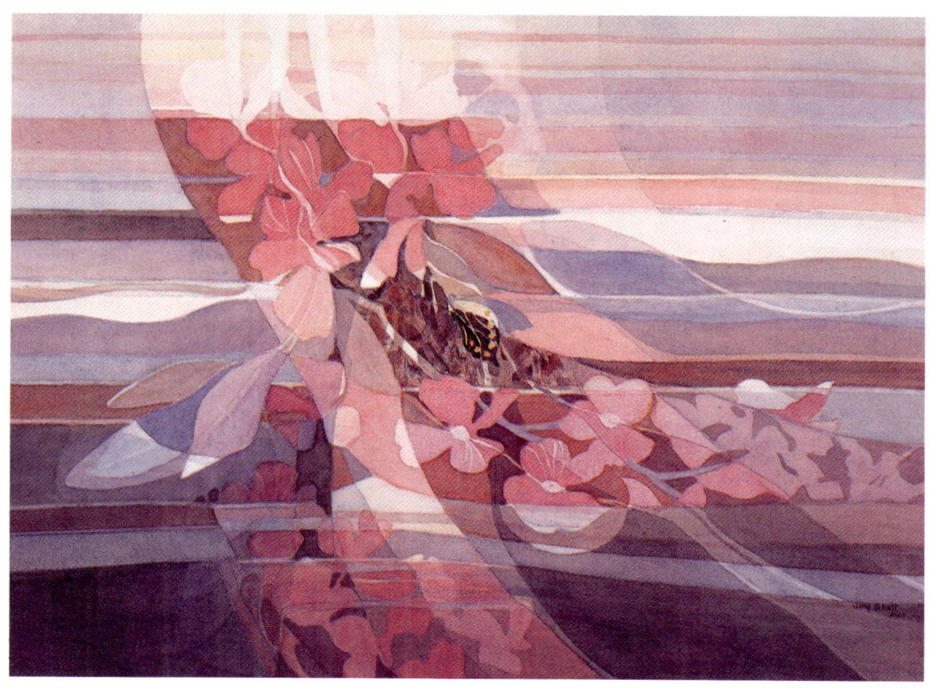

JOY SHOTT

Changing Light Winds
Watercolor
22 x 30 Inches

Connections of time, space, objects, light and gentle winds caused a shifting of blooms and leaves that transformed the tree into moving color patterns intertwined with pieces of light.

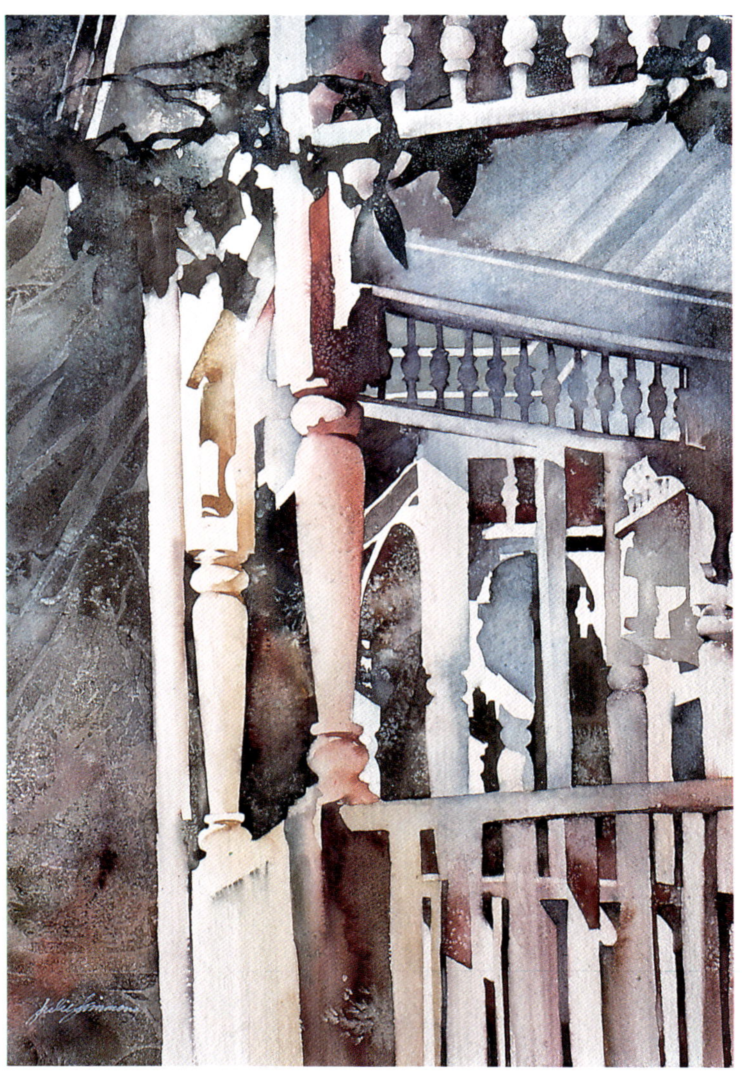

JULIE LUTZ SIMMONS

Victorian Vision
Watercolor
30 x 22 Inches

Man-made shapes interwoven with God-made patterns of light and shadow. Veils of color and texture lead us through layers of memories connecting past with present, the inner journey of man and the universe.

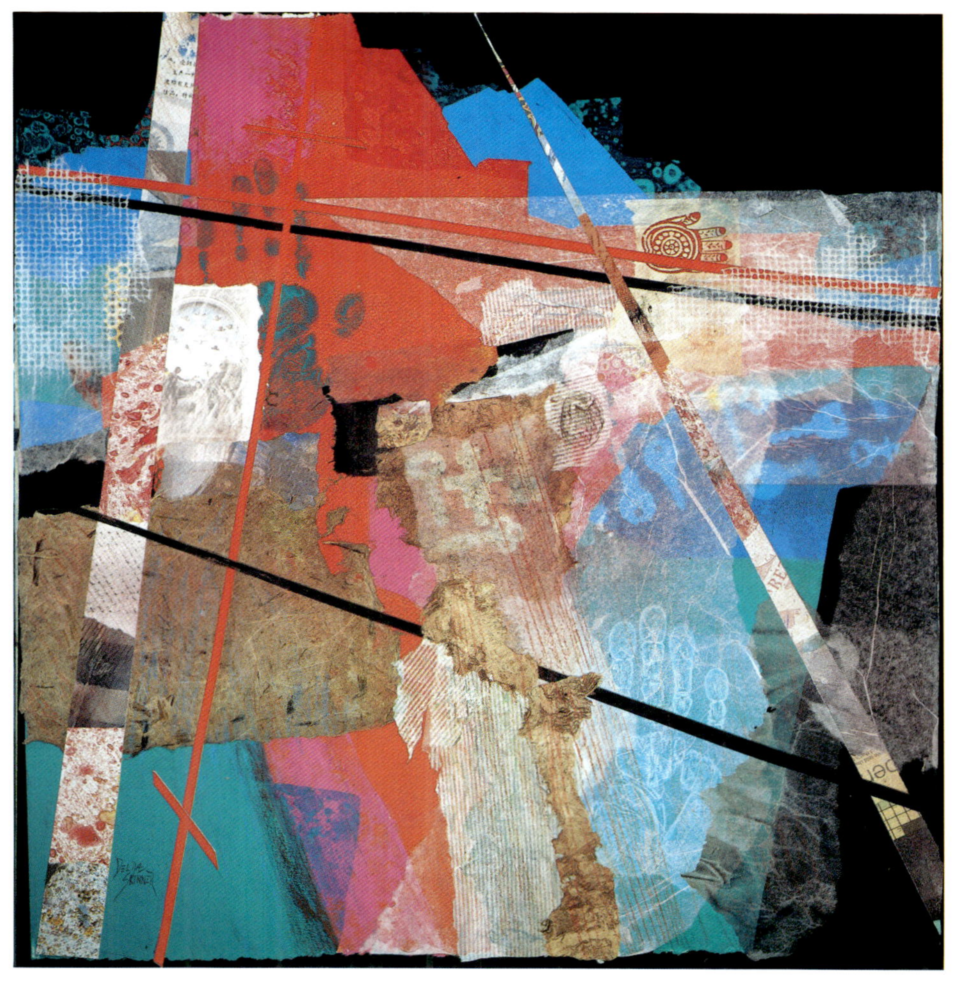

DELDA SKINNER

Coalescence
Collage: handmade and marblized papers, acrylic,
bark, frottage
22 x 21 Inches

*My work focuses on relationships. One color with
another, one symbol with another, one thought
imbued with another, the viewer with the painting.
These relationships coalesce to create an aura of
wholeness and truth.*

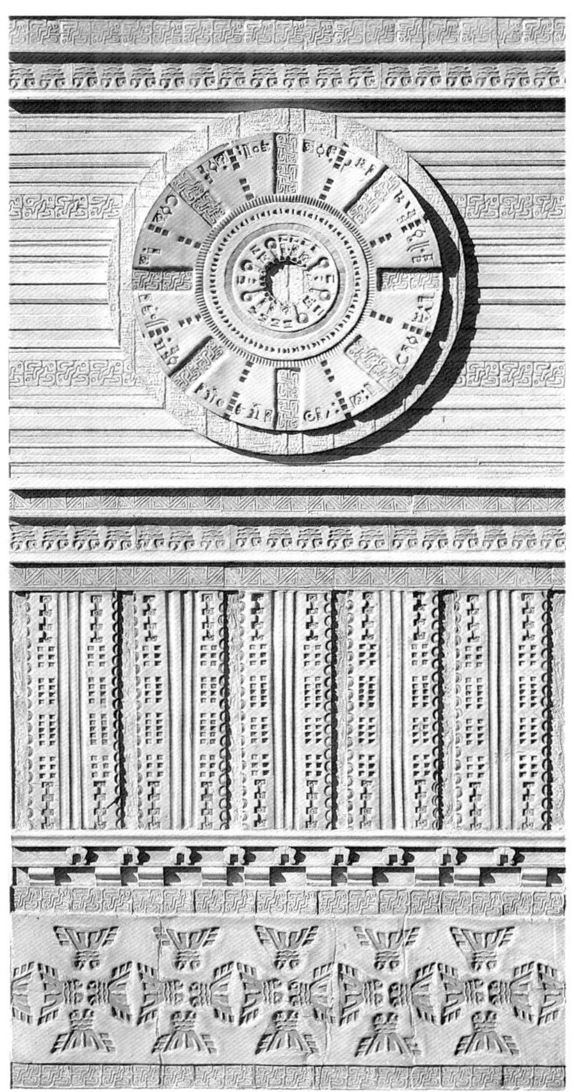

MARTHA SLAYMAKER

Metamorphosis
Porcelain, wood and mixed media on
plywood backing
76 x 38

In the remains of cultures far different in time and space, universal symbols linger on and some genetic healing images are retained....perhaps in my mind.

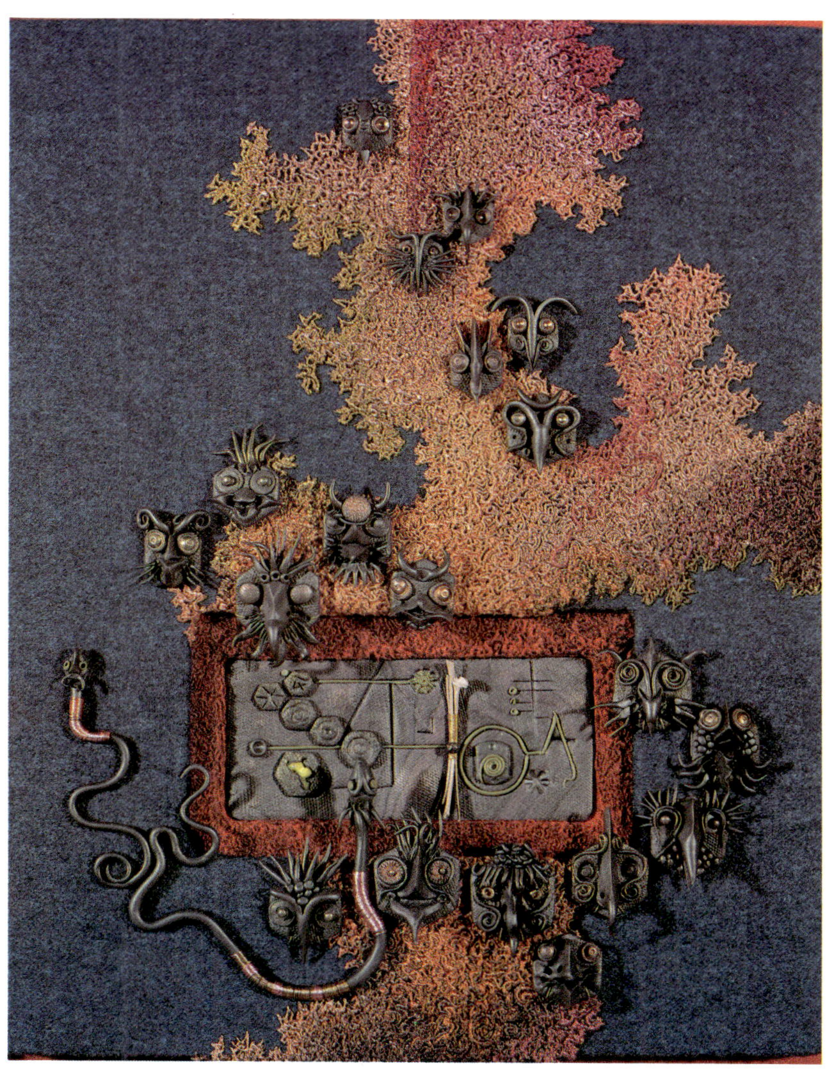

WILCKE H. SMITH

Cryptoglyph I
Mixed media: stitchery/polyform
14 1/2 x 11 3/4 x 2 Inches

"Cryptoglyph I" integrates clay and fiber in a stitchery/polyform fantasy of enigmatic marks and avian spirits. Its forms emerge from belief in ancient myths, powerful forces and quarks.

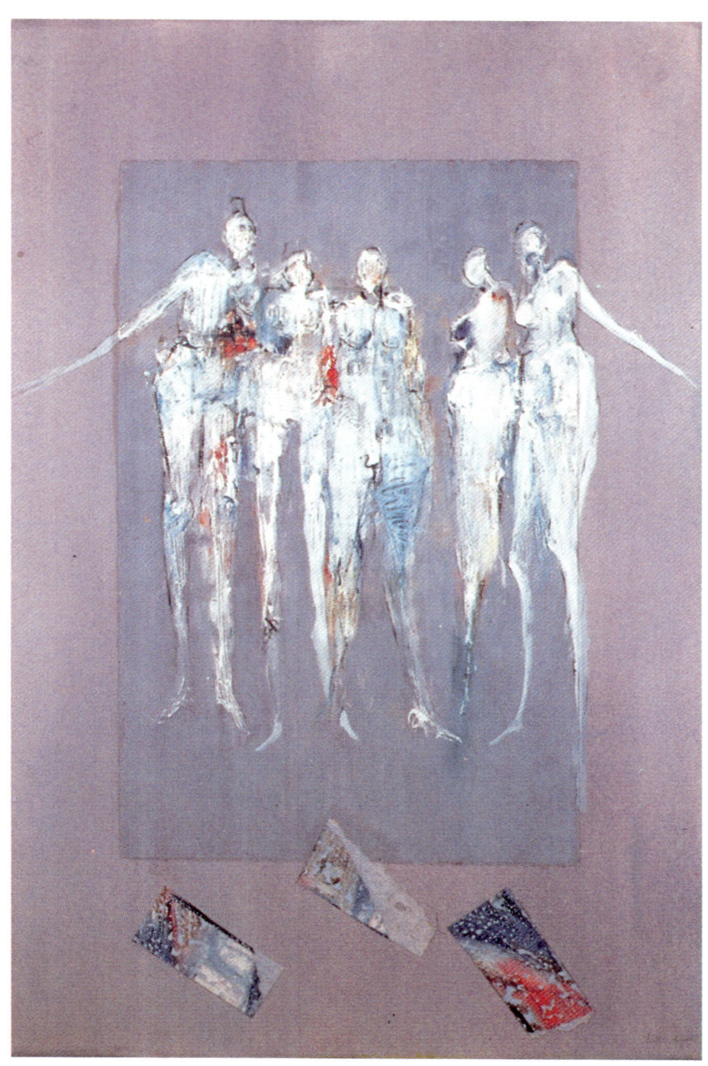

RUTH C. SNYDER

Five Figures
Mixed media
60 x 40 Inches

Layers: consciousness reaching downward into subconsciousness and into the soul - revealing at times human evolvement from distant past to present.

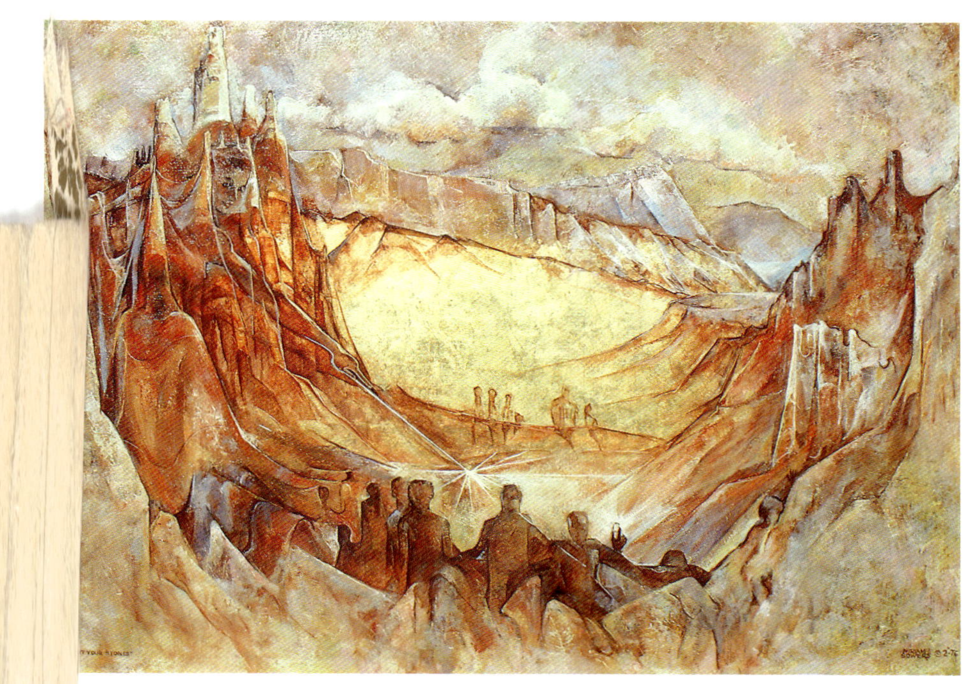

MIRIAM SOWERS

Cast Out Your Stones
Oil on gold leaf
36 x 48 Inches

My paintings always have people in them, subtley hidden in nature and sunshine. Titles are poetic suggestions, moral issues, spiritual symbols, prayer plea or prophecy...to promote healing thoughts.

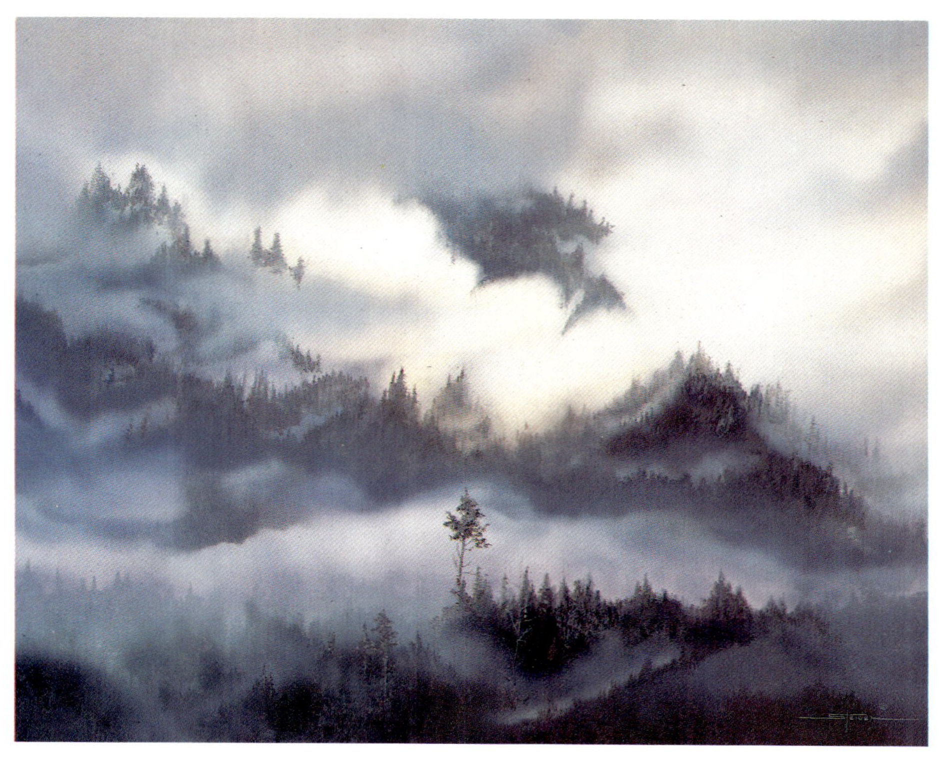

DORIS STEIDER

World of Illusion
Egg tempera
22 x 28 Inches

Art is life...or is it the other way around?
It is illusion. It is multiplicity of feelings and
sights and events drifted and layered over
and around and beneath consciousness.

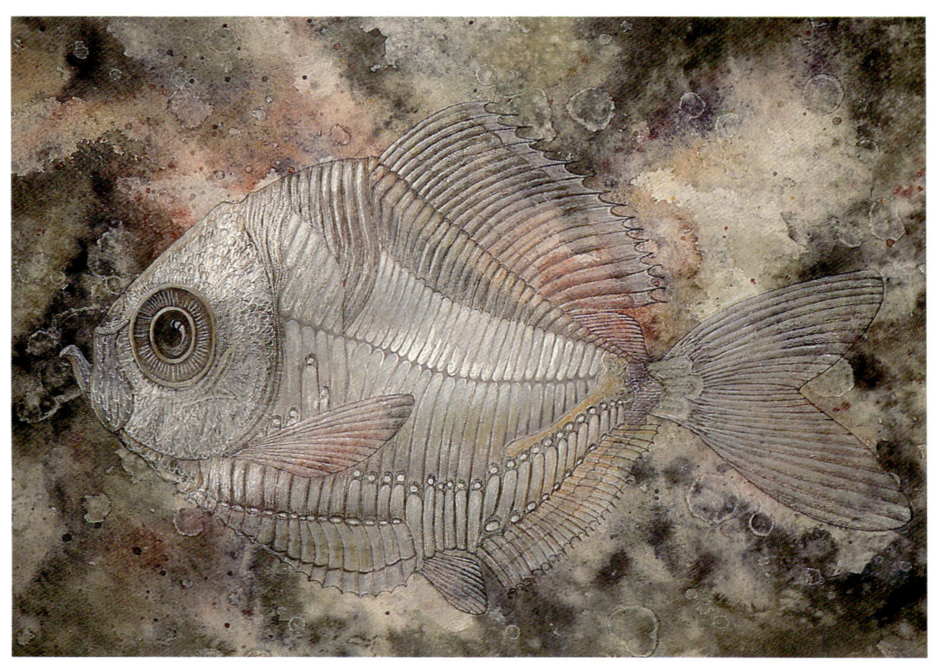

MARILYN STOCKER-SMITH

Ichthus III
Watercolor and colored pencil
16 x 20 Inches

"Ichthus III" was done in response to ancient fish forms. All are fanciful versions exploring alternate possibilities of evolution by myth or master plan.

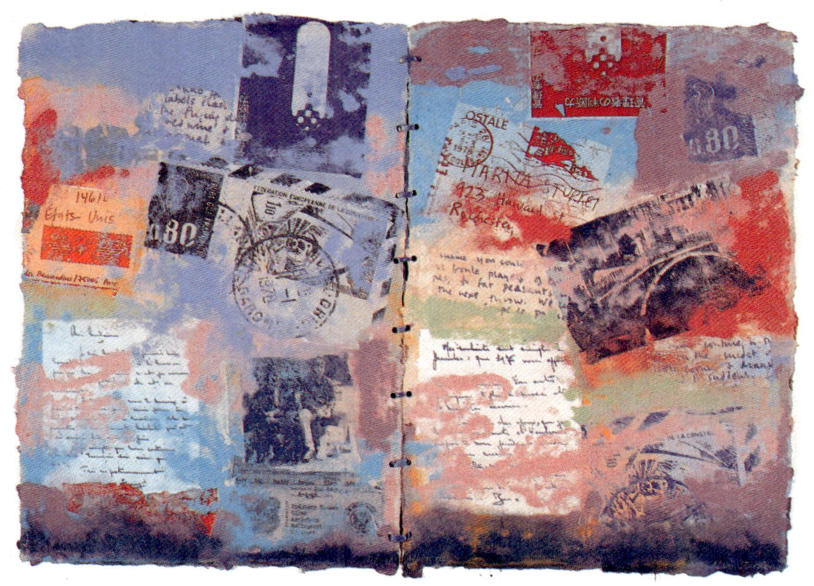

MARIE STURKEN

Travel Album III
Handmade paper
24 x 33 Inches

*I use paper pulp as a medium, color Japanese
silk tissues on my lithographic press, print photo-litho
plates with bits of personal history on them and
layer them into the wet pulp.*

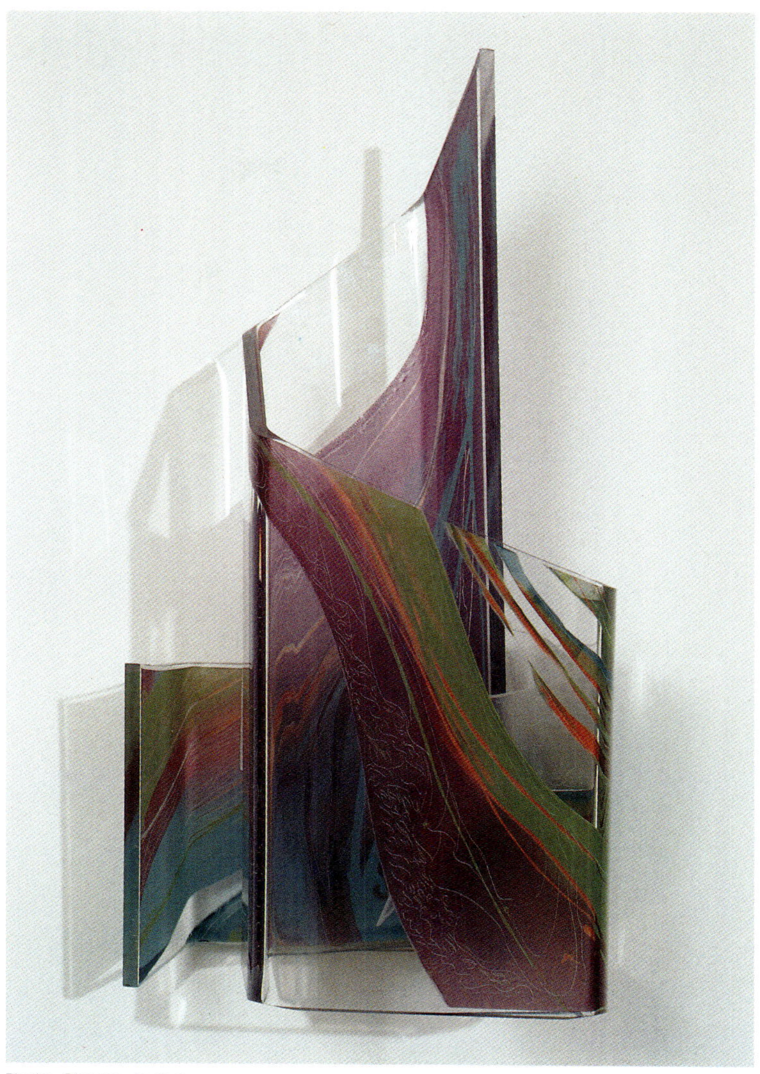

Photo: Damian Andrus

HILDA APPEL VOLKIN

Ceremonial Spiral
Low-relief acrylic wall sculpture
22 x 12 x 8 Inches

I paint with light. Inside "Ceremonial Spiral", the light is drawn inward and upward, the surfaces reflect the ceremonies of our life cycles.

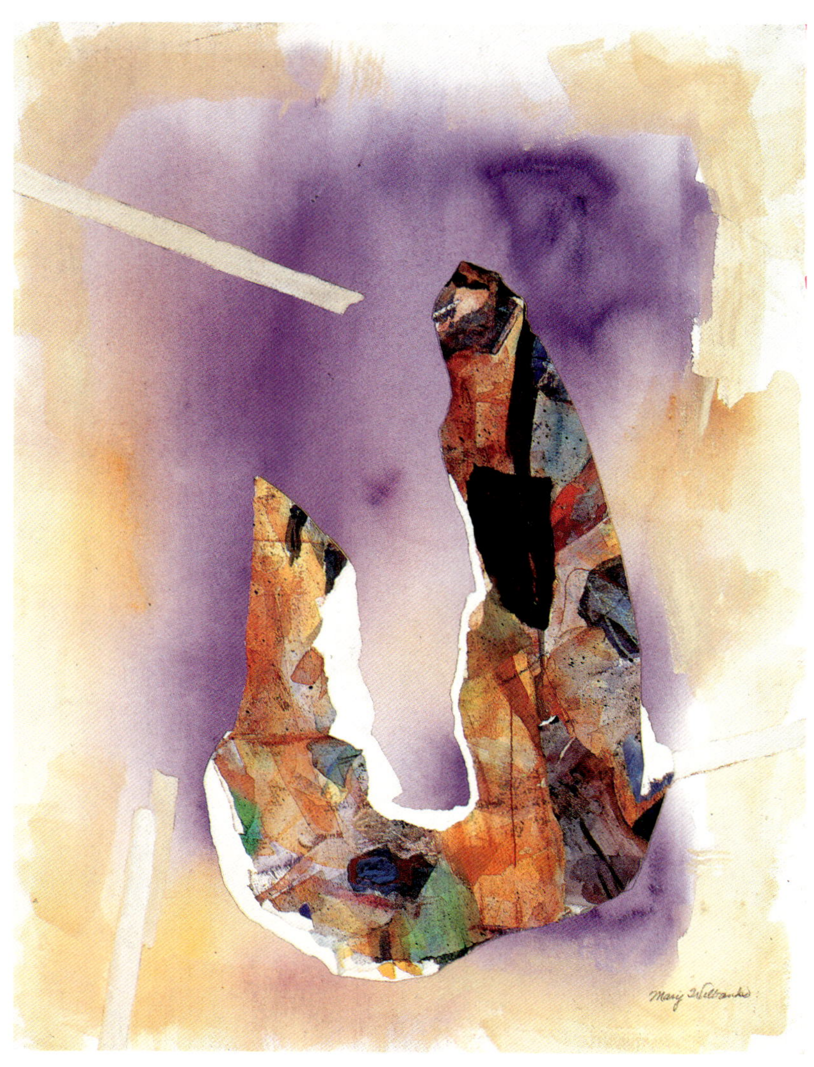

MARY WILBANKS

Silence Is Golden
Acrylic collage
30 x 22 Inches

My life and my layering is a process. Although my work does not deny the existence of a shadow or sorrow, it is life affirming work, and that is what I want it to reflect.

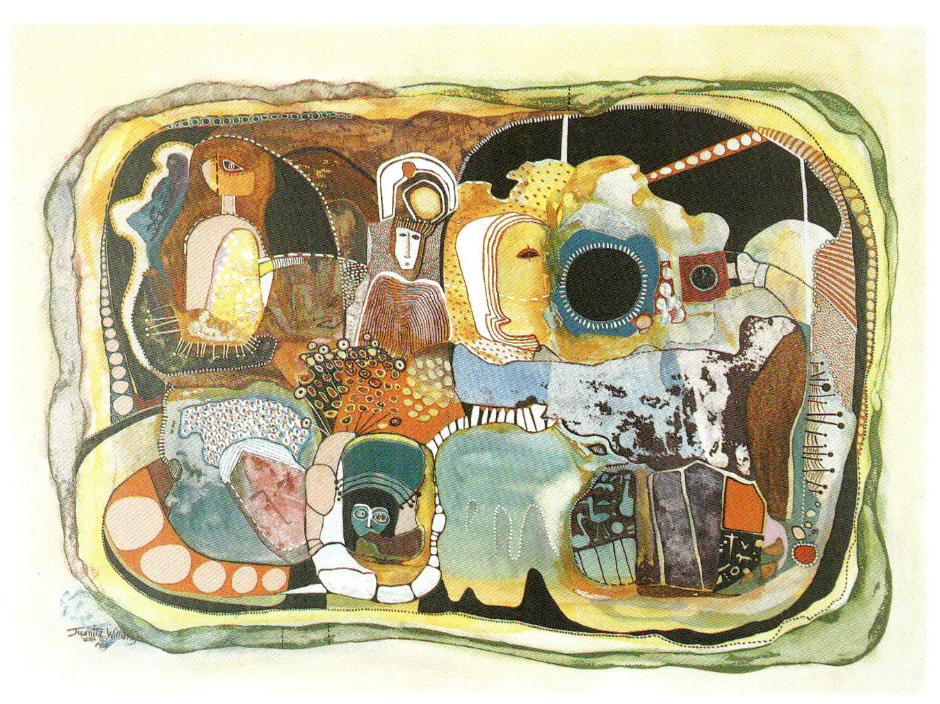

JUANITA WILLIAMS

Past Lives
Acrylic
30 x 40 Inches

*Layering is life...which is: time, thoughts,
deeds, caring, knowledge, dreams,
happiness, sadness, pain, love and death.
Perhaps there are layers before birth and
after death, never-ending.*

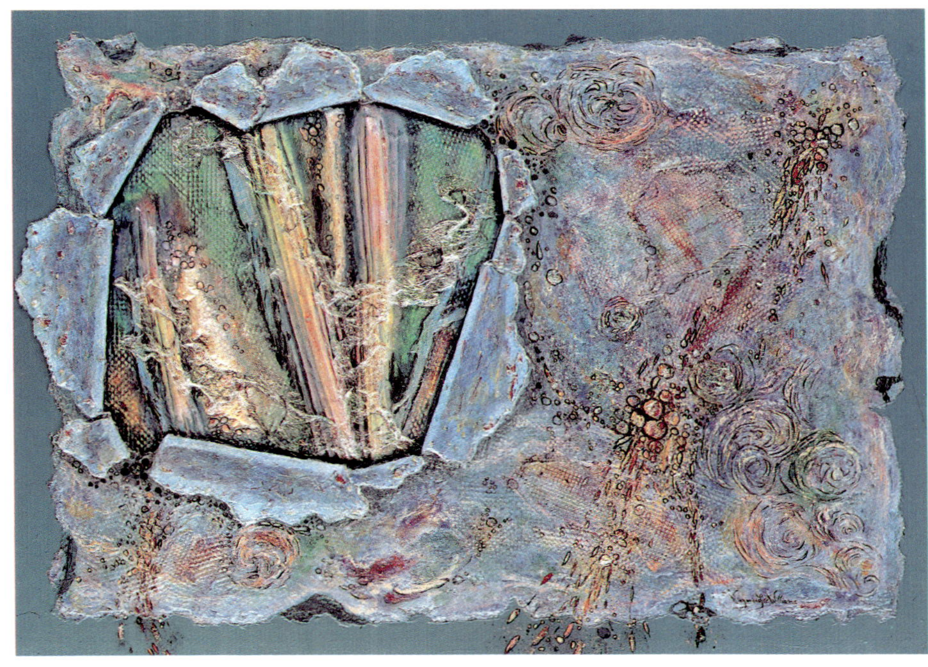

VIRGINIA LEE WILLIAMS

And to the Jewels of the Sea
Torn paper, acrylic and iridescent
plastic film
26 x 35 Inches

*As we peel back the layers of time we
unearth the beauty of the eons during
which creation has been developing
its wonderous format for the future of
the universe.*

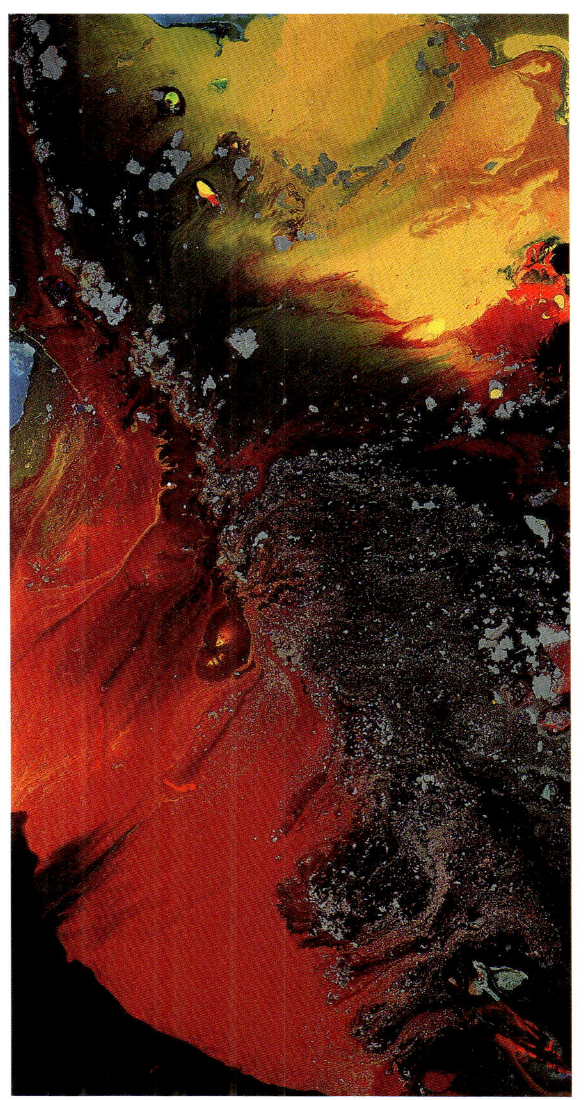

DIANA WONG

Galactic Sea #2
Acrylic/enamel
72 x 36 Inches

To create is to synchronize my energy with the universe in order to put my whole being into a grand perspective. My attempt is to see the whole and go beyond.

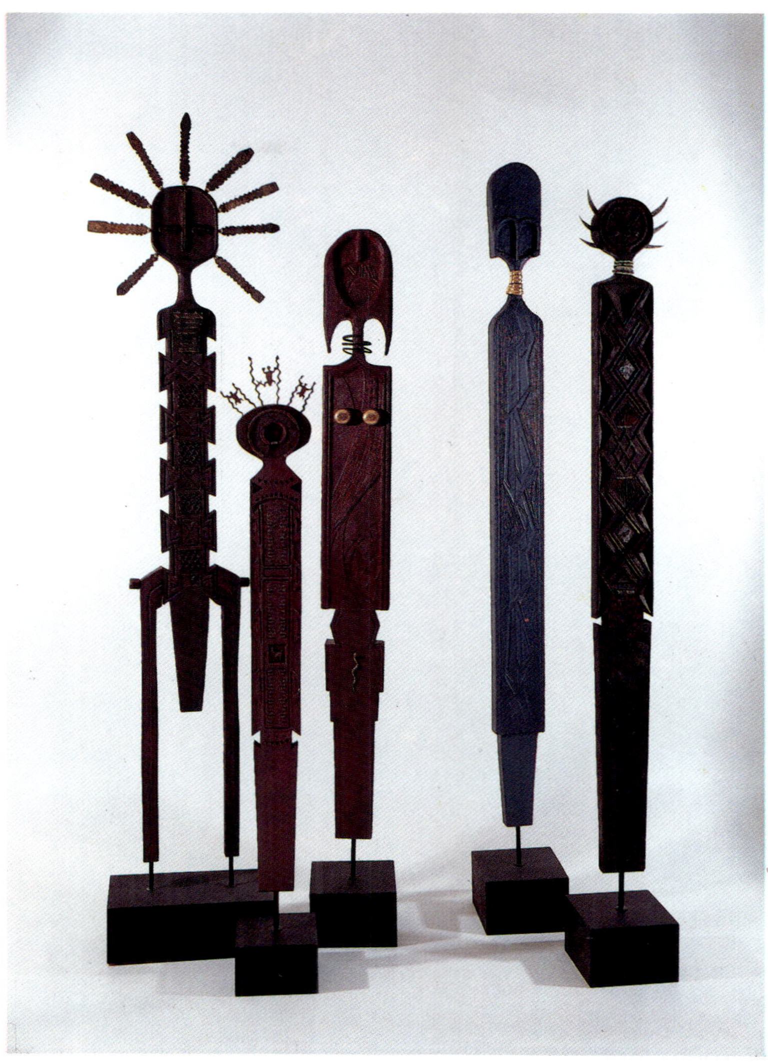

Photo: Tom Terries

NANCY AND ALLEN YOUNG

Spirit Guides
Mixed media: wood, metal, paper
78 x 8 x 8 Inches to 93 x 16 x 8 Inches

"Spirit Guides" reflect the collective consciousness
of all people. While we seek their contact in the
present , they bring illumination from the past
and an occasional glimpse of the future.

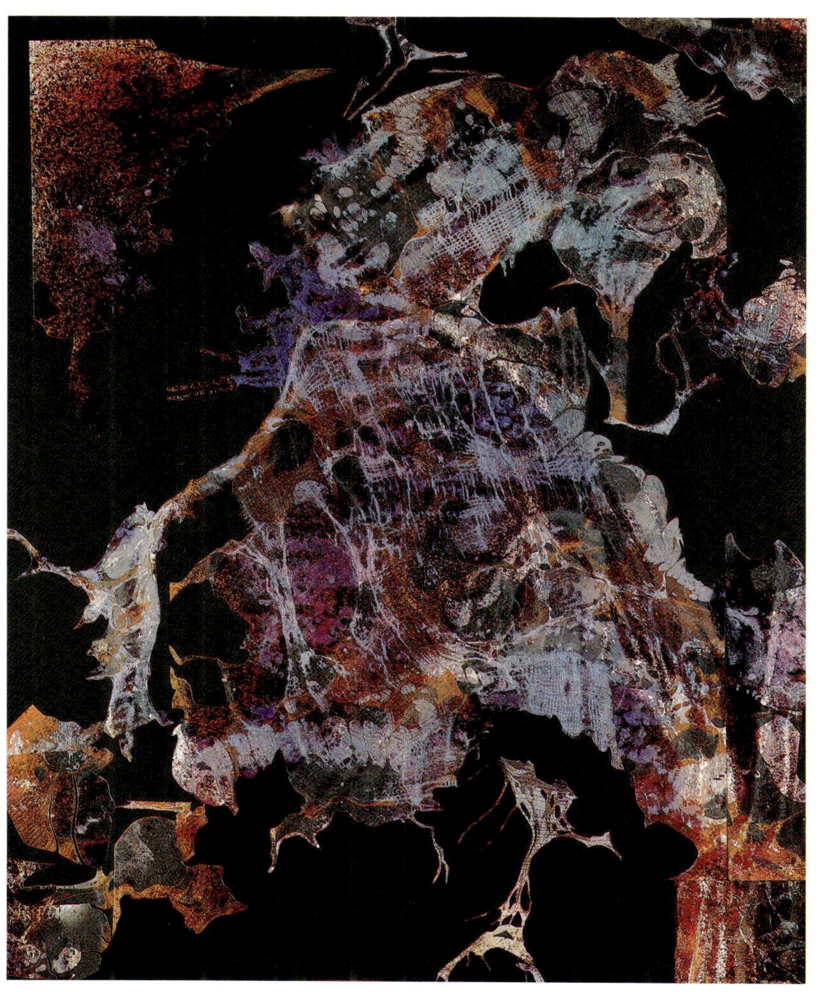

PAM BROOKS ZOHNER

The Translation
Mixed media
40 x 32 Inches

Dynamic are the powers of mind
That create through reason,
A seahorse
Translated from woven particles
Into melting layers of gauzy orbs
Growing, though devoured
by time, past and present.

INDEX OF ARTISTS

Markowitz, Marilyn, 124 Camino Bosque • Boulder, CO 80302
Martinez-Rodgers, Victoria, 1410 Goff Blvd SW • Albuquerque, NM 87110
Meredith, Ruth, 2916 La Veta NE • Albuquerque, NM 87110
Morris, Elaine W. 314 8th St. • Oakmont, PA 15139
Musick, Pat, P.O. Box 919 • Huntsville, AR 72740
Nagai, Ikuko, 26 Condon Court • San Mateo, CA 94403
Nelson, Mary Carroll, 1408 Georgia NE • Albuquerque, NM 87110
Newman, Richard, P.O. Box 162 • Bradford, MA 01835
Newman, Rochelle, P.O. Box 162 • Bradford, MA 01835
Phillis, Marilyn Hughey, 72 Stamm Circle • Wheeling, WV 26003
Ploski, Cynthia, 1460 Brierwood Court • Rio Rancho, NM 87124
Poduska, T.F., 10233 W. Powers Ave. • Littleton, CO 80127
Provder, Carl, 1416 Elva Terrace • Encinitas, CA 92024
Reynolds, Jeny, 5739 Bastille Pl. • Columbus, OH 43213
Ruyle, Lydia, 2101 24th St. • Greely, CO 80631
Shott, Joy, 1023 Groveland Dr. • Bluefield, WV 24701
Simmons, Julie Lutz, 10250 E. Mountain View #229 • Scottsdale, AZ 85258
Skinner, Delda, P.O. Box 707 • Wimberley, TX 78676
Slaymaker, Martha, 451 Gavilan Pl NW • Albuquerque, NM 87107
Smith, Wilcke H., 3616 Dakota NE • Albuquerque, NM 87110
Snyder, Ruth C., 550 Hanley Ave. • Los Angeles, CA 90049
Sowers, Miriam, 3020 Glenwood NW • Albuquerque, NM 87104
Steider, Doris, 30 Silver Hills Lane • Albuquerque, NM 87123
Stocker-Smith, Marilyn, 2077 Riggs Rd. NE • Newark, OH 43055
Sturken, Marie, 21 Bayberry Rd. #2 • Princeton, NJ 08540
Volkin, Hilda Appel, 8421 Aztec Rd NE • Albuquerque, NM 87111
Wilbanks, Mary, 18307 Champion Forest Dr. • Spring, TX 77379
Williams, Juanita R., 419 Longview Ave. • Zanesville, OH 43701
Williams, Virginia Lee, 329 Carthage Place • Trotwood, OH 45426
Wong, Diana, 1547 6th St. • Santa Monica, CA 90401
Young, Nancy and Allen, 11416 Brussels Ave. NE • Albuquerque, NM 87111
Zohner, Pam Brooks, 1725 W. Loma Lane • Phoenix, AZ 85021

THE SOCIETY OF LAYERISTS IN MULTI-MEDIA
1408 Georgia NE
Albuquerque, NM 87110

Library of Congress Catalog Card Number 91-60297

ISBN 0-9628851-0-X

Editor — Ann Hartley
Associate — Editor Delda Skinner
Designer — Pam Brooks Zohner
Cover — Arizona Graphic's Network
Printed in Bangkok, Thailand